The
Bread Machine Magic
Book of Helpful Hints

The
Bread Machine Magic
Book of Helpful Hints

✦✦✦

DOZENS OF PROBLEM-SOLVING HINTS
AND TROUBLESHOOTING TECHNIQUES
FOR GETTING THE MOST OUT OF
YOUR BREAD MACHINE

Linda Rehberg and Lois Conway

Illustrations by Durell Godfrey

ST. MARTIN'S PRESS
New York

Book design by Helene Berinsky

Library of Congress Cataloging-in-Publication Data

Rehberg, Linda
    The bread machine magic book of helpful hints / Linda Rehberg and
Lois Conway.
        p.   cm.
    ISBN 0-312-09759-X (pbk.)
    1. Bread.   2. Automatic bread machines.   I. Conway, Lois.
II. Title.
TX769.R383   1993
641.8'15—dc20   93-11453
                                                               CIP

First Edition: November 1993
10 9 8 7 6 5 4 3 2 1

This book is dedicated to Dennis and Jim,
two wonderful men who were born with twinkles in their eyes,
an Irish song in their souls, and
hearts quick and strong in their generous impulses.

"May the rocks in your field turn to gold."
—an old Irish toast

Contents

Acknowledgments   xi

Introduction   xiii

1. Bread Machines   1

The Various Bread Machine Features   1

    DAK   7

    HITACHI   10

    MAXIM   13

    MK SEIKO   14

    PANASONIC/NATIONAL   18

    REGAL   21

    SANYO   24

    TOASTMASTER   26

    TRILLIUM BREADMAN   28

    WELBILT   29

    WEST BEND   35

    ZOJIRUSHI   37

2. Bread-Baking Facts and Guide Lines   39

The Science and Art of Baking Bread   39

Essential Guidelines for Bread Machine Baking   43

Measurements/Conversions   47

3. Ingredients   49

Wheat Flours   49

Non-wheat Flours   54

Gluten-free Flours and Grains   56
Whole Grains   58
Yeast   65
Liquids   69
Fats   72
Salt   73
Sweeteners   73
Eggs   78
Gluten   79
Dough Enhancers   81
Sourdough   84
Miscellaneous Ingredients   87
Substitutions   90

4. How to Adjust Recipes to Fit Your Dietary Needs   95
The Nutritional Benefits of Homemade Bread   95
Ways to Reduce or Eliminate Fats in Bread   97
How to Reduce or Eliminate Sugar in Bread   98
Cutting the Salt in Half   99
Lowering the Cholesterol in Bread   100
High-fiber Breads   101
Breads for Animal Lovers   102
Wheat-free/Gluten-free Breads   104
Gene's Basic Rice Bread   106
Bob's Cheddar Cheese Bread   107
Melody's Brown and White Bread   108

5. Helpful Hints and Troubleshooting Techniques   109
Tips for Baking the Perfect Loaf   109
How to Adapt Your Favorite Recipes for the Bread Machine   114
The Next Step: How to Create Your Own Recipes   116
Home Milling   117
How to Counteract Troublesome Climatic Conditions   118
Adjustments for High-Altitude Bread Baking   119
Small Loaves: a Multitude of Causes and the Solutions   120
Sunken Loaves: What Went Wrong   125

Loaves That Have Mushroom Tops or Overflow:
How to Prevent Them   125
An Assortment of Common Problems: Their Causes and Cures   127
Refrigerating/Freezing Bread Dough   131
Storing Bread   133
Cleaning Your Machine   133
Our Favorite Accessories: The Little Extras That Add to the
Fun of Baking Homemade Bread   134

6. Recipes   139

San Diego Sunshine   141
DeDe's Buttermilk Bread   142
Anne and Bill's Apple Oatmeal Bread with Raisins   143
Herb Bread   144
Jim's Cinnamon Rolls   146
Whole Wheat Hamburger and Hot Dog Buns   148
Sweet Lelani Bread   150
Jalapeño Cheese Bread   151
Jim's Maple Walnut Bread   152
Linda's Lemon Bread   153
Buttermilk Honey Bran Bread   154
Jana's Seed and Nut Bread   154
Shayna's Vegan Burgers   156
French Bread Extraordinaire!   158
Quaker Multigrain Bread   160
Whole Wheat Cinnamon Raisin Bread   161
Lois's Country Crunch Bread   162
Herb Rolls   164
Chicken Broccoli Pockets   166
Dawn's Vanilla Raisin Bread   168
Sweet Milk Bread   170
Applesauce Rye Bread   171
Ann's Bierocks   172
Shareen's Whole Wheat Pizza Crust   174
Oatmeal Bread   176
Dennis's Multigrain Bread   177

Ham and Pepper Cheese Bread   178
Country Rye Breadsticks   180
Christy's Christmas Trees   182
Sour Rye Bread   185
Suggested Uses   186

7. Sources   189

Index   195
Coupon   205

Acknowledgments

Looking at the acknowledgment page in our last book, *Bread Machine Magic*, you would have thought we'd written The Great American Novel! We will try to contain ourselves this time. There are, however, many wonderful people who are a major part of this book. Most of them are former Prodigy members who have taken us many, many more steps down this road then we ever thought we'd travel. We hope that when you read this book you'll see how much their spirits are a part of it. We wish to acknowledge and thank Irwin Franzel, our favorite rocket scientist, "Zoji" bread baker, and friend. The depth of his knowledge, his willingness to respond to a daily barrage of questions, and his compassion for other human beings seems limitless. Linda Caldwell is another kindhearted human being who we've loved from the day she threatened to do a song-and-dance routine at our first cooking class in her tap shoes and Groucho glasses. Her charming personality radiates right through the video screen and she is always the first to lend a hand on the bulletin board when someone's having bread machine problems. We also send our many thanks to both Gene Hill and Melody Gabriel, who took so much time to answer all our questions on gluten-free breads and shared their favorite recipes with us. We've been very fortunate to meet and become friends with people like Susan Lipton, Diana Lewis, Christiane Stakely, Marianne Wright, and Michelle Cook. In addition to their many witty and humorous notes, they all shared helpful hints that were incorporated into this book. Many people passed through Prodigy's revolving door, shared their experiences, gave us valuable feedback, expanded our knowledge, and kept us on our toes. We wish to say "thank you" to all of you. Most of us have moved on to new Bulletin-Board Systems, but the "good ol' days" on Prodigy were certainly fun while they lasted.

We are very much indebted to Glenna Vance, who, on her own time, spent many hours running nutritional analyses of all our recipes.

Once again, we never would have made it through without Debbie and Rick Carlson's computer wisdom and patience in times of extreme stress to keep us up and running. Thank you both!

Ann Slaybaugh, Jim Bodle, and Dawn Fletcher . . . thanks for sharing and inspiring some great recipes!

We would also like to thank Ann Slaybaugh and Scott Parker, two very special teachers at Poway High School, for lending a hand with the math problems. Linda would still be trying to figure out those substitutions if it weren't for you!

Jana Cason, we are very grateful to you for nursing us along in our fledgling teaching careers. Your wonderful sense of humor, gentle guidance, and kind support meant a lot to us.

Two years have passed and we're still convinced that Barbara Anderson, our editor, is the best in the business! Barbara, your calm, soothing voice over the phone has been music to our ears in times of panic. We are very thankful for your insightful comments, direction, and unwavering support of our brainstorm. Marian Lizzi, we thank you, too, for being there for us with a smile.

There were lots of friends, co-workers, and neighbors who helped us out a great deal by taking all this bread off our hands. We always appreciated your comments and hope you'll be nearby when we start testing recipes for the next book.

Thank you, Shayna, for the impact your nature-loving, animal-preserving lifestyle has had on us. We're certain you'll contribute much more than Vegan Burgers to this world in your lifetime.

This certainly wouldn't be complete without mentioning the family pets . . . four very special testers: Peppy Rehberg and the Conway brood of Soft Coated Wheaten Terriers—Briscoe, Missy, and Susie. Theirs are discriminating palates indeed.

Our love and our gratitude are strongest felt for the two men in our lives, Jim and Dennis. Once again they endured countless nights without dinners, testy wives, kitchens torn up or turned into laboratories, and nonexistent social lives. The dust has settled, and it's great to see you're both still here.

Introduction

◆◆◆

The love affair continues. . . .

When we finished our first book, *Bread Machine Magic*, we thought our bread machine "career" was over. We moved all but our favorite machines to the garage, took a deep breath, and contemplated the many ways we would take some time off to kick back and relax. But what we discovered was that our first book was only the beginning. We were immediately caught up in a flurry of activities. We did numerous book signings, joined the Prodigy network, began teaching bread machine classes, and answered hundreds of phone calls and letters. Everyone had questions, questions, questions, and we didn't always have the answers! We had to pull out those dusty bread machines and go back to work. If we didn't find the answers in the kitchen, we headed for our local libraries. We attended cooking classes. It was obvious that our wonderful relationship with the bread machine wasn't over. It was simply blossoming into a new dimension.

We met, spoke, and communicated with hundreds of determined yet frustrated bread machine owners. At book signings and classes, strangers hugged and thanked us when we came up with solutions to their common problems. (We'll work for hugs any day!) Those who had purchased a bread machine because they didn't know the first thing about baking, seemed to be in need of basic information. The experienced bakers threw more difficult questions our way and always asked "Why?" It was in the middle of a book signing that the idea for this book finally bubbled to the surface. Though people encouraged us to write another cookbook, it was obvious that what they truly needed was the information we were teaching in our classes!

We scooped up all our teaching notes, jotted down the questions people asked, conducted endless tests, and at night fell asleep reading dozens of books to expand our basic understanding of the science and inexact art of baking bread. For several months, Linda typed morning, noon, and night, while Lois worked the phones.

Our sights were set on combining all we possibly could into one unique book, a handy reference guide for bread machine owners. People with special dietary needs constantly wanted to know how to eliminate or lower the fat, sugar, cholesterol, sodium, or animal products in their breads. "How does one adjust to adverse weather conditions or high-altitude baking?" people asked. Our favorite was the woman who wanted to know how to lighten up her breads. She claimed her breads were so dense and heavy that when the birds ate them, they fell out of the sky! We were asked if it was possible to bake breads in the machine free of wheat or gluten. We've answered these concerns to the best of our ability. It's our hope that you'll find this book a very useful kitchen companion and a helping hand. Baking homemade bread is meant to be a very simple pleasure. We wish that for you most of all.

Your questions spurred us on, kept us on our toes, and inspired this book. We feel much of it was written, in a sense, by all of you. Therefore, we'd like to end this introduction to your book with a few of our favorite quotes from the bread machine bakers on the Prodigy network. People like this are why we still have an ongoing love affair with bread machines and the wonderful people who use them.

> "My advice is to accept your current inabilities and bake, bake, bake. Every loaf I made was a learning experience in itself. Experiment and get the feel of the flours, the dough, and use as many senses as possible to learn to make the type of bread dearest to your heart."
>
> —BENJAMIN PRATER

> "The automatic bread machine is an example of using high tech to restore us to one of the simple pleasures of childhood. In honor of this paradox, I keep the bread machine sitting on top of an ancient foot-treadle sewing machine."
>
> —GINNIE SAMS

> "Bread touches a heartstring in our souls that reminds us of cold days and the warmth of a mother's touch and snuggling in close to the hearth."
>
> —KAREN DAY

The
Bread Machine Magic
Book of Helpful Hints

❖❖❖ **1** ❖❖❖

Bread Machines

The Various Bread Machine Features
❖❖❖

The two questions we're asked most often are: "Which bread machine is your favorite?" and "Which machine do you recommend?" While we're more than happy to rave about our favorites and can recommend several, it's far better if we help you become an informed buyer. The machine you take home should be one in your price range with features that *you*—not we—feel are essential.

So if you're an undecided prospective bread machine owner, befuddled by the multitude of options bread machines offer, read on. What follows is a brief description of the various features now available and a listing of all the bread machines currently on the market. We promise not to endorse any machine in particular, but simply to list each machine's specifications along with some helpful information. (The machine specifications were provided by the manu-facturers in nearly all cases.) Jot down those features you consider essential in the order of their priority. Through a process of elimination, you'll narrow your choices down to just one or two machines best suited for your needs.

When selecting a machine, keep in mind the servicing aspect. We want you to know we've baked thousands of loaves in our bread machines over the years and still haven't had to send any of them in for repairs; however, when your mixing blade has just been gobbled up by the garbage disposal, you're not going to appreciate hearing elevator music every time you dial the customer service number. Also, if you have a local appliance repair shop that handles bread machines, ask questions about the problems they see most often and how long it takes to order parts for the machine(s) you're considering.

One last note: don't be put off by the suggested retail prices we quote. In most cases, we've found the machines selling for considerably less, some-times more than 50 percent less! It pays to shop around, watch newspaper ads for sales, and ask questions of other bread machine owners. Lois purchased her machines through mail order. There's a wonderful book called *The Wholesale-by-Mail Catalogue*, by Lowell Miller and Prudence McCullough (New York: HarperCollins Publishers, 1992), that lists sources for many products. It's updated regularly.

LOAF SIZE

Basically, bread machines produce three different sizes of loaves: 1 pound; 1½ pounds; and 2 pounds (though if you were to weigh each loaf, the weight would rarely be accurate). The 1-pound loaf contains approximately two cups of flour, the 1½-pound loaf has about three cups of flour, and the 2-pound loaf uses four cups of flour.

The benefit of buying the larger 1½- or 2-pound machine is that, in most cases, you have the option of making the smaller loaf as well. For just one or two people, however, sometimes the smaller 1-pound machine makes more sense. Since the breads contain no artificial preservatives, they usually remain fresh for only two or three days. You're better off making smaller loaves more often than making a large loaf that takes a week to consume. (It gives you the opportunity for more variety, too).

LOAF SHAPE

There are three shapes of loaves currently available: round; vertically rectangular (similar to a loaf of store-bought bread stood on end); and hori-zontally rectangular (these bear the closest resemblance to homemade bread baked in a regular bread pan).

There are advantages to all three shapes. The round loaf is very versatile. Sliced vertically, each slice looks "normal"; sliced horizontally, you'll have round bread (nice if you're feeling a bit whimsical); sliced vertically down the center and then each half sliced horizontally, you produce half rounds to fit in the toaster.

The most common bread machine shape is the vertically rectangular loaf (which includes the more square-shaped 1-pound loaf). When turned on its side and sliced, every slice is consistently the same size (approximately a 4¾-inch square). If your bread doesn't rise very tall one time or hits the lid the next time, you'll still have the same size slice of bread, just fewer or more of them, whichever the case may be. For that reason, the vertically rectangular pan allows you to bake the loaf size of your choice.

The horizontally rectangular pan produces the most attractive loaf, perfect for gift giving. If it weren't for the telltale hole in the bottom, you could take all the credit for such a wonderful bread.

PREHEAT CYCLE

Some machines will warm the ingredients either prior to mixing or during the kneading phase. There's no need to spend the extra time bringing your ingredients to room temperature if your machine does it for you prior to mixing.

RAPID BAKE CYCLE

This cycle bakes bread approximately one hour faster than the Regular Bake cycle. It's also referred to as a Quick Bake or Turbo cycle. The duration of the Regular Bake cycle varies widely from machine to machine; some are 3½ to 4 hours, others as short as 2¼ hours. Therefore, some bread machines list no Rapid Bake cycle but their standard baking cycle may actually be a Rapid Bake (which we consider to be anything under 3 hours).

DOUGH (OR MANUAL) CYCLE

This feature signals you to remove the dough at the stage where it's ready to be shaped, allowed to rise one last time, and then baked. Almost every machine has this option and it's one we've learned to enjoy more and more. It's also very beguiling for experienced, hands-on bread bakers who have lovingly crafted many a loaf of bread over the years but can now appreciate new choices: a fresh loaf of homemade bread that takes only five minutes to create or the more leisurely, familiar process of working with the dough again, shaping it as desired, and baking it in the oven.

WHOLE WHEAT CYCLE

This cycle extends the kneading and rising phases, which is a boon for breads that contain at least 50 percent whole-grain flours. Can you bake whole-grain breads in machines without this feature? Yes. Without the extended cycles, however, sometimes you need to compensate by adjusting your ingredients, adding gluten, or stopping and restarting your machine after the first kneading cycle—all in an effort to achieve taller, lighter, whole-grain loaves.

FRENCH BREAD CYCLE

This cycle is best suited for breads low in fat and sugar. Usually, less time is spent kneading the dough and more time is devoted to the rising cycle, which results in breads with crisp, crackly crusts and coarse, chewy interiors. You can produce crisp-crusted breads in machines that do not have this feature by eliminating the fat and reducing the sugar in your recipes. Such loaves won't be identical to those baked on a French Bread cycle, however.

SWEET BREAD CYCLE

Some machines offer this feature in addition to offering a crust color selector. It's best suited for breads that are high in sugar or fat (more than 2 tablespoons) or breads that burn easily, such as egg, cheese, and some whole-grain breads. In most cases, your bread will bake at a lower temperature. In other machines, it's also a longer cycle, start-to-finish, than the standard cycle.

RAISIN/NUT CYCLE

This feature comes in handy when you want to bake a bread with raisins, chopped dried fruits, or nuts. The machine will signal late in the kneading phase when it's time to add the extras. It prevents them from being pulverized, which can happen if they're added in the very beginning with the rest of the ingredients. It's been our experience, however, that not every machine and not every recipe results in "smooshed" raisins, liquified dried fruits, or nonexistent nuts.

JAM/RICE/CAKES/QUICK BREADS

These are options available on the "deluxe" machines. Some people dismiss them at first, but once they stop and think about slathering a thick slice of their warm, fresh-baked bread with some delicious homemade jam or marmalade, this feature becomes much more enticing!

Quick breads (not to be confused with breads baked on a Rapid Bake cycle) are non-yeast breads such as banana nut bread, pumpkin bread, etc. A very limited number of machines offer the Cake and/or Quick-Bread cycle.

The Hitachi B201 is the only bread machine that has the rice-cooking feature.

COOL-DOWN CYCLE

Though it won't cool the bread completely after baking, this half-hour cycle will remove excessive heat and moisture from the machine so you won't be left with a soggy, limp loaf in case you're not around when the baking ends.

You'll notice that instead of a Cool-Down cycle, some machines do the opposite and keep the bread warm for an hour after baking ends.

DELAYED BAKE TIMER

Undoubtedly, this is the most popular bread machine feature of all. It allows you to program your machine to bake at a specified time, which means you can wake to the heady aroma of freshly baked bread (could there be a better alarm clock?) or be greeted by an intoxicating fragrance as you walk through the door after work. For that reason, this feature is standard on almost every machine.

VIEWING WINDOW

We've baked thousands of loaves and we still like to "sneak a peek." Actually, the window isn't the frill it might seem to be at first. When you're trying a bread recipe for the first time, it's wise to check it several times during the kneading phase. If it appears too wet or too dry, you can make adjustments and avoid disappointing results four hours later. It also enables you to spot the dough that is threatening to overflow the bread pan the moment the baking cycle kicks on. (A mere prick with a toothpick will prevent certain disaster.) Conversely, with only moments left in the rising cycle, it will also reveal the sad news that the loaf you planned to give as a gift will be only four inches tall.

One last benefit of the viewing window, and one that we've never seen written up in any of the instruction booklets, is that it's a dandy way to entertain visiting grandchildren!

CRUST COLOR SELECTION

We find that most machines on the default Medium Crust setting bake up breads that are a little too dark for our liking. We opt for the Light setting most of the time, especially when baking whole-grain loaves, breads high in sugar, or breads containing eggs or cheese. Fortunately, the majority of bread machines give you the opportunity to select your preferred crust color.

POWER SAVER

If you live in an area that experiences frequent power outages, this feature may be your savior. If your electricity goes off or someone pulls the cord on your bread machine, all is not lost. If power is restored within ten minutes, your machine will pick up right where it left off. (If not, simply remove the dough, place it in a greased 8 × 4 inch (1-pound loaf) or 9 × 5 inch (1½-pound loaf) bread pan, allow it to rise until doubled, then bake "the old-fashioned way.")

YEAST DISPENSER

Some Panasonic/National machines have a small compartment in the lid that dispenses the yeast shortly before the second kneading phase rather than adding it in the beginning with the rest of the ingredients. The yeast dispenser guarantees that the yeast will remain dry and not activate prematurely when using the Delayed Bake setting. Since the yeast is separated from the rest of the ingredients, the machine is able to mix the yeast-free dough the moment you press Start, even on the Delayed Timer. This unique feature enables you to judge and make adjustments to *all* bread doughs, not just those that are baked immediately.

✦✦✦

DAK AUTO BAKERY

Loaf Size: 1½-Pound
Loaf Shape: Round
Suggested Retail Price: $129.90

Cycles:

Preheat	yes	French Bread	yes
(During the first Kneading cycle)		Raisin/Nut	yes
Rapid Bake	no	Jam/Rice	no
Dough/Manual	yes	Cake/Quick Bread	no
Whole Wheat	no	Cool Down	yes

Other Features:

Delayed Bake Timer	yes	Crust Color Selection	yes
Viewing Window	yes	Power Saver	no

Other: **Sweet Bread cycle for recipes high in sugar, fat, or eggs**

Customer Service Phone Number
1-818-888-5373 (hotline)
1-800-888-6703 (TDD for the hearing impaired)

HINTS ON PRODUCING THE BEST LOAVES
WITH THIS BREAD MACHINE:

• Use room-temperature ingredients.

• Listen to your machine as it kneads. If it sounds like the motor is straining because the dough is too stiff, add 1 to 2 tablespoons more liquid.

• If your recipes contain more than 2 tablespoons of sweetener, are high in fat or eggs, or bake up too dark, use the Sweet Bread setting.

• If any breads are not fully cooked on top, next time cover the glass dome with a piece of aluminum foil to retain more heat. (Take care not to cover the air vents around the edge.)

• After the first kneading cycle, most doughs are well kneaded. If you are in a hurry, you can remove your pizza dough or dinner roll dough after the first kneading/rising phase (1¼ hours) rather than wait for it to knead and rise a second time (the complete Manual cycle).

• To prevent the machine from scooting off the counter, place a skid-proof material such as a typewriter pad underneath it.

• You can remove the hot paddle from the loaf with a crochet hook or a pair of chopsticks.

DAK TURBO BAKER II

Loaf Size: 1½-Pound
Loaf Shape: Round
Suggested Retail Price: $163.90

Cycles:

Preheat	**yes**	French Bread	**yes**
(During the first Kneading cycle)		Raisin/Nut	**yes**
Rapid Bake	**yes**	Jam/Rice	**no**
Dough/Manual	**yes**	Cake/Quick Bread	**no**
Whole Wheat	**no**	Cool Down	**yes**

Other Features:

Delayed Bake Timer	**yes**	Crust Color Selection	**yes**
Viewing Window	**yes**	Power Saver	**no**

Other: **Sweet Bread cycle for recipes high in sugar, fat, or eggs**

Customer Service Phone Number:
1-818-888-5373 (hotline)
1-800-888-6703 (TDD for the hearing impaired)

HINTS ON PRODUCING THE BEST LOAVES WITH THIS BREAD MACHINE:

• Use room-temperature ingredients.

• Listen to your machine as it kneads. If it sounds like the motor is straining because the dough is too stiff, add 1 to 2 tablespoons more liquid.

• If your recipes contain more than 2 tablespoons of sweetener, are high in fat or eggs, or bake up too dark, use the Sweet Bread setting.

• If any breads are not fully cooked on top, next time cover the glass dome with a piece of aluminum foil to retain more heat. (Take care not to cover the air vents around the edge.)

• After the first kneading cycle, most doughs are well kneaded. If you are in a hurry, you can remove your pizza dough or dinner roll dough after the first kneading/rising phase (1¼ hours) rather than wait for it to knead and rise a second time (the complete Manual cycle).

• To prevent the machine from scooting off the counter, place a skid-proof material such as a typewriter pad underneath it.

• You can remove the hot paddle from the loaf with a crochet hook or a pair of chopsticks.

DAK TURBO BAKER IV

Loaf Size: 2-Pound
Loaf Shape: Round
Suggested Retail Price: $183.90

Cycles:

Preheat	**yes**	French Bread	**yes**
(During the first Kneading cycle)		Raisin/Nut	**yes**
Rapid Bake	**yes**	Jam/Rice	**no**
Dough/Manual	**yes**	Cake/Quick Bread	**no**
Whole Wheat	**yes**	Cool Down	**yes**

Other Features:

Delayed Bake Timer	**yes**	Crust Color Selection	**yes**
Viewing Window	**yes**	Power Saver	**no**

Other: **Oat Bread Cycle**

Customer Service Phone Number:
1-818-888-5373 (hotline)
1-800-888-6703 (TDD for the hearing impaired)

HINTS ON PRODUCING THE BEST LOAVES WITH THIS BREAD MACHINE:

• Use room-temperature ingredients.

• Listen to your machine as it kneads. If it sounds like the motor is straining because the dough is too stiff, add 1 to 2 tablespoons more liquid.

• If any breads are not fully cooked on top, next time cover the glass dome with a piece of aluminum foil to retain more heat. (Take care not to cover the air vents around the edge.)

• After the first kneading cycle, most doughs are well kneaded. If you are in a hurry, you can remove your pizza dough or dinner roll dough after the first kneading/rising phase (1¼ hours) rather than wait for it to knead and rise a second time (the complete Manual cycle).

• To prevent the machine from scooting off the counter, place a skid-proof material such as a typewriter pad underneath it.

• You can remove the hot paddle from the loaf with a crochet hook or a pair of chopsticks.

HITACHI HB-B101

Loaf Size: ½-Pound, 1-Pound, 1½-Pound
Loaf Shape: Vertically Rectangular
Suggested Retail Price: $329.95

Cycles:

Preheat	yes	French Bread	no
(During the second Kneading		Raisin/Nut	yes
cycle)		Jam/Rice	no
Rapid Bake	yes	Cake/Quick Bread	no
Dough/Manual	yes	Cool Down	yes
Whole Wheat	no		

Other Features:

Delayed Bake Timer	yes	Crust Color Selection	yes
Viewing Window	yes	Power Saver	yes

Other: **Convection cooking and cool down. "Lock" that keeps the program from being accidentally canceled.**

Customer Service Phone Number:
1-800-241-6558, extensions 720, 719

HINTS ON PRODUCING THE BEST LOAVES WITH THIS BREAD MACHINE:

• All ingredients should be at room temperature; water should be 90°–120°F.

• If the bread crust is too dark, even on the light setting, try cutting back a tiny bit on the sugar.

• Keep both the bottom of the bread pan and the pan sensor inside the machine clean.

HITACHI HB-B201

Loaf Size: ½-Pound, 1-Pound, 1½-Pound
Loaf Shape: Vertically Rectangular
Suggested Retail Price: $349.95

Cycles:

Preheat	yes	French Bread	no
(During the second Kneading		Raisin/Nut	yes
cycle)		Jam/Rice	yes
Rapid Bake	yes	Cake/Quick Bread	no
Dough/Manual	yes	Cool Down	yes
Whole Wheat	no		

Other Features:

Delayed Bake Timer	yes	Crust Color Selection	yes
Viewing Window	yes	Power Saver	yes

Other: **Convection cooking and cool down. "Lock" that keeps the program from accidentally being canceled.**

Customer Service Phone Number:
1-800-241-6558, extensions 720, 719

HINTS ON PRODUCING THE BEST LOAVES WITH THIS BREAD MACHINE:

• All ingredients should be at room temperature; water should be 90°–120°F.

• If the bread crust is too dark, even on the light setting, try cutting back a tiny bit on the sugar.

• Keep both the bottom of the bread pan and the pan sensor inside the machine clean.

HITACHI HB-B301

Loaf Size: ½-Pound, 1-Pound, 1½-Pound, 2-Pound
Loaf Shape: Vertically Rectangular
Suggested Retail Price: $399.95

Cycles:

Preheat	**yes**	French Bread	**no**
(During the second Kneading		Raisin/Nut	**yes**
cycle)		Jam	**yes**
Rapid Bake	**yes**	Rice	**no**
Dough/Manual	**yes**	Cake/Quick Bread	**yes**
Whole Wheat	**no**	Cool Down	**yes**

Other Features:

Delayed Bake Timer	**yes**	Crust Color Selection	**yes**
Viewing Window	**yes**	Power Saver	**yes**

Other: **Convection cooking and cool down. "Lock" that keeps the program from accidentally being canceled.**

Customer Service Phone Number:
1-800-241-6558, extensions 720, 719

HINTS ON PRODUCING THE BEST LOAVES WITH THIS BREAD MACHINE:

• All ingredients should be at room temperature; water should be 90°–120°F.

• If the bread crust is too dark, even on the light setting, try cutting back a tiny bit on the sugar.

• Keep both the bottom of the bread pan and the pan sensor inside the machine clean.

MAXIM ACCU BAKERY BB-1

Loaf Size: 1-Pound
Loaf Shape: Vertically Rectangular
Suggested Retail Price: $200.00

Cycles:

Preheat	no	Raisin/Nut	yes
Rapid Bake	yes	Jam/Rice	no
Dough/Manual	yes	Cake/Quick Bread	no
Whole Wheat	yes	Cool Down	no
French Bread	yes		

Other Features:

Delayed Bake Timer	yes	Crust Color Selection	yes
Viewing Window	no	Power Saver	no

Other: **This machine also has a Rye Bread cycle**

Salton/Maxim provides a consumer hotline for bread machine owners.

Customer Service Phone Number:
1-800-233-9054

MK SEIKO MR. LOAF HB-12W

Loaf Size: 1-Pound
Loaf Shape: Vertically Rectangular
Suggested Retail Price: $299.95

Cycles:

Preheat	no	Raisin/Nut	no
Rapid Bake	yes	Jam/Rice	no
Dough/Manual	yes	Cake/Quick Bread	no
Whole Wheat	no	Cool Down	yes
French Bread	yes	*(1-Hour Keep Warm cycle)*	

Other Features:

Delayed Bake Timer	yes	Crust Color Selection	no
Viewing Window	no	Power Saver	yes

Other: **Sweet Bread cycle for recipes high in sugar, fat, or eggs**

HINTS ON PRODUCING THE BEST LOAVES WITH THIS BREAD MACHINE:

• Using the 3 hour 40 minute French Bread or Sweet Bread cycles will often result in taller loaves.

MK SEIKO MR. LOAF HB-210

Loaf Size: 1-Pound
Loaf Shape: Vertically Rectangular
Suggested Retail Price: $249.95

Cycles:

Preheat	no	French Bread	yes
Rapid Bake	no	Raisin/Nut	no
(But full cycle is 2 hours 20		Jam/Rice	no
minutes—essentially a Rapid		Cake/Quick Bread	no
Bake)		Cool Down	yes
Dough/Manual	yes	*(1-Hour Keep Warm cycle)*	
Whole Wheat	no		

Other Features:

Delayed Bake Timer	yes	Crust Color Selection	yes
Viewing Window	no	Power Saver	yes

Other: **Sweet Bread cycle for recipes high in sugar, fat, or eggs**

HINTS ON PRODUCING THE BEST LOAVES WITH THIS BREAD MACHINE:

• Using the 3 hour 40 minute French Bread or Sweet Bread cycles will often result in taller loaves.

MK SEIKO MR. LOAF HB-211

Loaf Size: 1-Pound
Loaf Shape: Vertically Rectangular
Suggested Retail Price: $179.95

Cycles:

Preheat	no	French Bread	no
Rapid Bake	no	Raisin/Nut	no
(But full cycle is 2 hours 20		Jam/Rice	no
minutes—essentially a Rapid		Cake/Quick Bread	no
Bake)		Cool Down	yes
Dough/Manual	yes	*(1-Hour Keep Warm cycle)*	
Whole Wheat	no		

Other Features:

Delayed Bake Timer	no	Crust Color Selection	no
Viewing Window	no	Power Saver	yes

MK SEIKO MR. LOAF/CHEFMATE HB-215

Loaf Size: 1-Pound, 1½-Pound
Loaf Shape: Vertically Rectangular
Suggested Retail Price: $299.95

Cycles:

Preheat	no	French Bread	yes
Rapid Bake	no	Raisin/Nut	no
(But full cycle is 2 hours 30		Jam/Rice	no
minutes—essentially a Rapid		Cake/Quick Bread	no
Bake)		Cool Down	yes
Dough/Manual	yes	*(1-Hour Keep Warm cycle)*	
Whole Wheat	no		

Other Features:

Delayed Bake Timer	yes	Crust Color Selection	yes
Viewing Window	no	Power Saver	yes

Other: **Sweet Bread cycle for recipes high in sugar, fat, or eggs**

HINTS ON PRODUCING THE BEST LOAVES WITH THIS BREAD MACHINE:

• Using the 3 hour 40 minute French Bread or Sweet Bread cycles will often result in taller loaves.

PANASONIC/NATIONAL SD-BT10P

Loaf Size: 1-Pound
Loaf Shape: Vertically Rectangular
Suggested Retail Price: $221.95

Cycles:

Preheat	no	Raisin/Nut	no
Rapid Bake	yes	Jam/Rice	no
Dough/Manual	yes	Cake/Quick Bread	no
Whole Wheat	yes	Cool Down	no
French Bread	no		

Other Features:

Delayed Bake Timer	yes	Crust Color Selection	yes
Viewing Window	no	Power Saver	yes

Customer Service Phone Number:
1-800-447-4700 (24-hour hotline)

PANASONIC/NATIONAL SD-BT55P/N

Loaf Size: 1-Pound
Loaf Shape: Vertically Rectangular
Suggested Retail Price: $259.95

Cycles:

Preheat	no	Raisin/Nut	no
Rapid Bake	yes	Jam/Rice	no
Dough/Manual	yes	Cake/Quick Bread	no
Whole Wheat	yes	Cool Down	no
French Bread	no		

Other Features:

Delayed Bake Timer	yes	Crust Color Selection	yes
Viewing Window	no	Power Saver	yes

Other: **Yeast dispenser in the lid of the machine**

Customer Service Phone Number:
1-800-447-4700 (24-hour hotline)

HINTS ON PRODUCING THE BEST LOAVES WITH THIS BREAD MACHINE:

• If you wish to open the lid to check the dough, do so while it is kneading or after the yeast has dropped. Do not open the lid between kneading cycles when the yeast is programmed to drop.

PANASONIC/NATIONAL SD-BT65P/N

Loaf Size: 1½-Pound
Loaf Shape: Horizontally Rectangular
Suggested Retail Price: $399.95

Cycles:

Preheat	no	Raisin/Nut	no
Rapid Bake	yes	Jam/Rice	no
Dough/Manual	yes	Cake/Quick Bread	yes
Whole Wheat	yes	Cool Down	no
French Bread	yes		

Other Features:

Delayed Bake Timer	yes	Crust Color Selection	yes
Viewing Window	no	Power Saver	yes

Other: **Yeast dispenser in the lid of the machine. This machine also has Crisp Dough, Whole Wheat Dough, and Variety Bread cycles.**

Customer Service Phone Number:
1-800-447-4700 (24-hour hotline)

HINTS ON PRODUCING THE BEST LOAVES WITH THIS BREAD MACHINE:

• If you wish to open the lid to check the dough, do so while it is kneading or after the yeast has dropped. Do not open the lid between kneading cycles when the yeast is programmed to drop.

• It may be necessary to push some of the ingredients out of the corners with a rubber spatula during the mixing cycle to ensure proper blending.

• A unique feature of this machine is that you can also prepare dough on the delayed timer.

• Occasionally, you will have a "ski slope" bread (one end of the loaf is much higher than the other). You can prevent this by checking the loaf during the rising cycle. If the dough is pushed to one side of the machine, gently spread it out with a rubber spatula.

REGAL KITCHEN PRO K6773

Loaf Size: 1-Pound, 1½-Pound
Loaf Shape: Vertically Rectangular
Suggested Retail Price: $349.95

Cycles:

Preheat	**no**	French Bread	**yes**
Rapid Bake	**no**	*(3 Hours 40 Minutes)*	
(But full cycle is 2 hours 30		Raisin/Nut	**no**
minutes—essentially a Rapid		Jam/Rice	**no**
Bake)		Cake/Quick Bread	**no**
Dough/Manual	**yes**	Cool Down	**yes**
Whole Wheat	**no**	*(1-Hour Keep Warm cycle)*	

Other Features:

Delayed Bake Timer	**yes**	Crust Color Selection	**yes**
Viewing Window	**no**	*(1½-Pound loaf only)*	
		Power Saver	**no**

Other: **Sweet Bread cycle for recipes high in sugar, fat, or eggs.**

Regal Breadmaker owners are given a toll-free number to call for assistance.

HINTS ON PRODUCING THE BEST LOAVES WITH THIS BREAD MACHINE:

• For the best whole-grain breads, stop then restart the machine after 15 minutes of kneading. The extra kneading cycle produces a better-textured, higher loaf.

REGAL K6774

Loaf Size: 1-Pound
Loaf Shape: Vertically Rectangular
Suggested Retail Price: $308.95

Cycles:

Preheat	no	Whole Wheat	no
Rapid Bake	no	French Bread	no
(but full cycle is 2 hours 20		Raisin/Nut	no
minutes—essentially a Rapid		Jam/Rice	no
Bake)		Cake/Quick Bread	no
Dough/Manual	yes	Cool Down	no

Other Features:

Delayed Bake Timer	no	Crust Color Selection	no
Viewing Window	no	Power Saver	no

Other: **Regal Breadmaker owners are given a toll-free number to call for assistance.**

HINTS ON PRODUCING THE BEST LOAVES WITH THIS BREAD MACHINE:

• For the best whole-grain breads, stop then restart the machine after 15 minutes of kneading. The extra kneading cycle produces a better-textured, higher loaf.

• When the room temperature is lower than 50°F, warm liquids to 100°F.

REGAL K6775

Loaf Size: 1-Pound, 1½-Pound
Loaf Shape: Vertically Rectangular
Suggested Retail Price: $349.95

Cycles:

Preheat	no	French Bread	yes
Rapid Bake	no	*(3 hours 40 minutes)*	
(But full cycle is 2 hours 30		Raisin/Nut	no
minutes—essentially a Rapid		Jam/Rice	no
Bake)		Cake/Quick Bread	no
Dough/Manual	yes	Cool Down	yes
Whole Wheat	no	*(1-Hour Keep Warm cycle)*	

Other Features:

Delayed Bake Timer	yes	Crust Color Selection	yes
Viewing Window	no	*(1½-Pound loaf only)*	
		Power Saver	no

Other: **Sweet Bread cycle for recipes high in sugar, fat, or eggs.**

Regal Breadmaker owners are given a toll-free number to call for assistance.

HINTS ON PRODUCING THE BEST LOAVES WITH THIS BREAD MACHINE:

• For the best whole-grain breads, stop then restart the machine after 15 minutes of kneading. The extra kneading cycle produces a better-textured, higher loaf.

SANYO BREAD FACTORY SBM-11

Loaf Size: 1-Pound
Loaf Shape: Vertically Rectangular
Suggested Retail Price: $229.99

Cycles:

Preheat	no	Raisin/Nut	no
Rapid Bake	no	Jam/Rice	no
Dough/Manual	yes	Cake/Quick Bread	no
Whole Wheat	no	Cool Down	yes
French Bread	no		

Other Features:

Delayed Bake Timer	yes	Crust Color Selection	no
Viewing Window	yes	Power Saver	no

Other: **Prepackaged bread mixes especially formulated for Sanyo Bread Machines are available.**

Customer Service Phone Number:
1-818-998-7322

SANYO BREAD FACTORY PLUS SBM-12

Loaf Size: 1-Pound
Loaf Shape: Vertically Rectangular
Suggested Retail Price: $299.99

Cycles:

Preheat	no	Raisin/Nut	no
Rapid Bake	yes	Jam/Rice	no
Dough/Manual	yes	Cake/Quick Bread	no
Whole Wheat	yes	Cool Down	yes
French Bread	yes		

Other Features:

Delayed Bake Timer	yes	Crust Color Selection	yes
Viewing Window	yes	Power Saver	yes

Other: **Sweet Bread cycle for recipes high in sugar, fat, or eggs**

Prepackaged bread mixes especially formulated for Sanyo Bread Machines are available.

Customer Service Phone Number:
1-818-998-7322

TOASTMASTER BREAD BOX 1150

Loaf Size: 1¼-Pound
Loaf Shape: Vertically Rectangular
Suggested Retail Price: $200.00

Cycles:

Preheat	no	Raisin/Nut	yes
Rapid Bake	yes	Jam/Rice	no
Dough/Manual	yes	Cake/Quick Bread	no
Whole Wheat	no	Cool Down	yes
French Bread	no	*(3-Hour Keep Warm cycle)*	

Other Features:

Delayed Bake Timer	yes	Power Saver	yes
Viewing Window	no	*(5 Seconds)*	
Crust Color Selection	yes		

Other: **One package of bread machine mix is included.**

Customer Service Phone Number:
1-800-947-3744

TOASTMASTER BREAD BOX 1151

Loaf Size: 1¼-Pound
Loaf Shape: Vertically Rectangular
Suggested Retail Price: $225.00

Cycles:

Preheat	**no**	Raisin/Nut	**yes**
Rapid Bake	**yes**	Jam/Rice	**no**
Dough/Manual	**yes**	Cake/Quick Bread	**no**
Whole Wheat	**no**	Cool Down	**yes**
French Bread	**no**	*(3-Hour Keep Warm cycle)*	

Other Features:

Delayed Bake Timer	**yes**	Power Saver	**yes**
Viewing Window	**no**	*(5 Seconds)*	
Crust Color Selection	**yes**		

Other: **Two packages of bread machine mix and a bread knife are included.**

Customer Service Phone Number:
1-800-947-3744

TRILLIUM BREADMAN TR-500

Loaf Size: 1-Pound, 1½-Pound
Loaf Shape: Vertically Rectangular
Suggested Retail Price: $299.00

Cycles:

Preheat	no	Raisin/Nut	yes
Rapid Bake	yes	Jam/Rice	no
Dough/Manual	yes	Cake/Quick Bread	no
Whole Wheat	yes	Cool Down	yes
French Bread	yes		

Other Features:

Delayed Bake Timer	yes	Crust Color Selection	yes
Viewing Window	yes	Power Saver	no

Other: **The Breadman also comes with: 3 prepackaged bread machine mixes, 3-year warranty, a video tape, *The Breadman's Healthy Bread Book*, and a 6-month nutrition hotline.**

Customer Service Phone Number:
1-800-800-8455

HINTS ON PRODUCING THE BEST LOAVES WITH THIS BREAD MACHINE:

• After placing ingredients in the baking pan, wait 10 minutes before pressing Start, or use the timer to add 10 minutes.

WELBILT ABM 100

Loaf Size: 1½-Pound
Loaf Shape: Round
Suggested Retail Price: $199.99

Cycles:

Preheat	**yes**	French Bread	**yes**
(During the first Kneading cycle)		Raisin/Nut	**yes**
Rapid Bake	**no**	Jam/Rice	**no**
Dough/Manual	**yes**	Cake/Quick Bread	**no**
Whole Wheat	**no**	Cool Down	**yes**

Other Features:

Delayed Bake Timer	**yes**	Crust Color Selection	**yes**
Viewing Window	**yes**	Power Saver	**no**

Other: **Sweet Bread cycle for recipes high in sugar, fat, or eggs**

Customer Service Phone Number:
1-516-365-5040

HINTS ON PRODUCING THE BEST LOAVES
WITH THIS BREAD MACHINE:

• Use room-temperature ingredients.

• Listen to your machine as it kneads. If it sounds like the motor is straining because the dough is too stiff, add 1 to 2 tablespoons more liquid.

• If your recipes contain more than 2 tablespoons of sweetener, are high in fat or eggs, or bake up too dark, use the Sweet Bread setting.

• If any breads are not fully cooked on top, next time cover the glass dome with a piece of aluminum foil to retain more heat. (Take care not to cover the air vents around the edge.)

• After the first kneading cycle, most doughs are well kneaded. If you are in a hurry, you can remove your pizza dough or dinner roll dough after the first kneading/rising phase (1¼ hours) rather than wait for it to knead and rise a second time (the complete Manual cycle).

• To prevent the machine from scooting off the counter, place a skid-proof material such as a typewriter pad underneath it.

• You can remove the hot paddle from the loaf with a crochet hook or a pair of chopsticks.

WELBILT ABM 150R MULTILOGIC

Loaf Size: 2-Pound
Loaf Shape: Round
Suggested Retail Price: $350.00

Cycles:

Preheat	yes	French Bread	no
(During the first Kneading cycle)		Raisin/Nut	yes
Rapid Bake	yes	Jam/Rice	no
Dough/Manual	yes	Cake/Quick Bread	yes
Whole Wheat	no	Cool Down	yes
(But you can program the machine for longer Kneading and Rising cycles)			

Other Features:

Delayed Bake Timer	yes	Crust Color Selection	yes
Viewing Window	yes	Power Saver	no

Other: **Also mixes cookie, pie, and pasta doughs**

Customer Service Phone Number:
1-516-365-5040

HINTS ON PRODUCING THE BEST LOAVES WITH THIS BREAD MACHINE:

• Use room temperature ingredients.

• Listen to your machine as it kneads. If it sounds like the motor is straining because the dough is too stiff, add 1 to 2 tablespoons more liquid.

• If any breads are not fully cooked on top, next time cover the glass dome with a piece of aluminum foil to retain more heat. (Take care not to cover the air vents around the edge.)

• After the first kneading cycle, most doughs are well kneaded. If you are in a hurry, you can remove your pizza dough or dinner roll dough after the first kneading/rising phase (1¼ hours) rather than wait for it to knead and rise a second time (the complete Manual cycle).

• To prevent the machine from scooting off the counter, place a skid-proof material such as a typewriter pad underneath it.

• You can remove the hot paddle from the loaf with a crochet hook or a pair of chopsticks.

WELBILT ABM 300/350

Loaf Size: 1-Pound
Loaf Shape: Round
Suggested Retail Price: $149.99

Cycles:

Preheat	**yes**	Whole Wheat	**no**
(During the first Kneading cycle)		French Bread	**no**
Rapid Bake	**no**	Raisin/Nut	**yes**
(But full cycle is 2 hours 10		Jam/Rice	**no**
minutes—essentially a Rapid		Cake/Quick Bread	**no**
Bake)		Cool Down	**no**
Dough/Manual	**yes**		

Other Features:

Delayed Bake Timer	**yes**	Crust Color Selection	**yes**
Viewing Window	**no**	Power Saver	**no**

Customer Service Phone Number:
1-516-365-5040

HINTS ON PRODUCING THE BEST LOAVES
WITH THIS BREAD MACHINE:

• Use room-temperature ingredients.

• Listen to your machine as it kneads. If it sounds like the motor is straining because the dough is too stiff, add 1 to 2 tablespoons more liquid.

• You can remove the hot paddle from the loaf with a crochet hook or a pair of chopsticks.

WELBILT ABM 500/550

Loaf Size: 1-Pound
Loaf Shape: Round
Suggested Retail Price: $199.99

Cycles:

Preheat	**yes**	Whole Wheat	**no**
(During the first Kneading cycle)		French Bread	**no**
Rapid Bake	**no**	Raisin/Nut	**yes**
(But full cycle is 2 hours 10		Jam/Rice	**no**
minutes—essentially a Rapid		Cake/Quick Bread	**yes**
Bake)		Cool Down	**no**
Dough/Manual	**yes**		

Other Features:

Delayed Bake Timer	**yes**	Crust Color Selection	**yes**
Viewing Window	**no**	Power Saver	**no**

Other: **Sweet Bread cycle for recipes high in sugar, fat, or eggs**

Customer Service Phone Number:
1-516-365-5040

HINTS ON PRODUCING THE BEST LOAVES WITH THIS BREAD MACHINE:

• Use room-temperature ingredients.

• Listen to your machine as it kneads. If it sounds like the motor is straining because the dough is too stiff, add 1 to 2 tablespoons more liquid.

• If your recipes contain more than 2 tablespoons of sweetener, are high in fat or eggs, or bake up too dark, use the Sweet Bread setting.

• You can remove the hot paddle from the loaf with a crochet hook or a pair of chopsticks.

WELBILT ABM 600

Loaf Size: 1-Pound
Loaf Shape: Round
Suggested Retail Price: $99.99

Cycles:

Preheat	**yes**	Whole Wheat	**no**
(During the first Kneading cycle)		French Bread	**yes**
Rapid Bake	**no**	Raisin/Nut	**yes**
(But full cycle is 2 hours 15		Jam/Rice	**no**
minutes—essentially a Rapid		Cake/Quick Bread	**no**
Bake)		Cool Down	**no**
Dough/Manual	**yes**		

Other Features:

Delayed Bake Timer	**no**	Crust Color Selection	**yes**
Viewing Window	**no**	Power Saver	**no**

Customer Service Phone Number:
1-516-365-5040

HINTS ON PRODUCING THE BEST LOAVES WITH THIS BREAD MACHINE:

• Use room-temperature ingredients.

• Listen to your machine as it kneads. If it sounds like the motor is straining because the dough is too stiff, add 1 to 2 tablespoons more liquid.

• You can remove the hot paddle from the loaf with a crochet hook or a pair of chopsticks.

WELBILT ABM 800

Loaf Size: 1-Pound
Loaf Shape: Round
Suggested Retail Price: $279.99

Cycles:

Preheat	**yes**	Whole Wheat	**yes**
(During the first Kneading cycle)		French Bread	**no**
Rapid bake	**no**	Raisin/Nut	**yes**
(But full cycle is 2 hours 10		Jam/Rice	**no**
minutes—essentially a Rapid		Cake/Quick Bread	**yes**
Bake)		Cool Down	**no**
Dough/Manual	**yes**		

Other Features:

Delayed Bake Timer	**yes**	Crust Color Selection	**yes**
Viewing Window	**yes**	Power Saver	**no**

Customer Service Phone Number:
1-516-365-5040

HINTS ON PRODUCING THE BEST LOAVES WITH THIS BREAD MACHINE:

• Use room-temperature ingredients.

• Listen to your machine as it kneads. If it sounds like the motor is straining because the dough is too stiff, add 1 to 2 tablespoons more liquid.

• You can remove the hot paddle from the loaf with a crochet hook or a pair of chopsticks.

WEST BEND BREAD AND DOUGH MAKER

41030

Loaf Size: 1-Pound, 1½-Pound
Loaf Shape: Vertically Rectangular
Suggested Retail Price: $333.25

Cycles:

Preheat	yes	Raisin/Nut	yes
Rapid Bake	yes	Jam/Rice	no
Dough/Manual	yes	Cake/Quick Bread	no
Whole Wheat	yes	Cool Down	yes
French Bread	yes		

Other Features:

Delayed Bake Timer	yes	Crust Color Selection	yes
Viewing Window	yes	Power Saver	no

Other: **Removable cover for easy cleaning. "Too Hot" and "Too Cold" feature prevents starting of machine if temperature of unit is not right for good results. Instructional video and starter bread mix included. The only bread machine company manufacturing machines in the U.S.A. This model is sold exclusively at Wal-Mart.**

Customer Service Phone Number:
1-800-367-0111

WEST BEND BREAD AND DOUGH MAKER

41040

Loaf Size: 1-Pound, 1½-Pound
Loaf Shape: Vertically Rectangular
Suggested Retail Price: $333.25

Cycles:

Preheat	yes	Raisin/Nut	yes
Rapid Bake	yes	Jam/Rice	no
Dough/Manual	yes	Cake/Quick Bread	no
Whole Wheat	yes	Cool Down	yes
French Bread	yes		

Other Features:

Delayed Bake Timer	yes	Crust Color Selection	yes
Viewing Window	yes	Power Saver	no

Other: **Removable cover for easy cleaning. "Lock" that keeps the program from accidentally being cancelled. "Too Hot" and "Too Cold" feature prevents starting of machine if temperature of unit is not right for good results. Instructional video and starter bread mix included. The only bread machine company manufacturing machines in the U.S.A.**

Customer Service Phone Number:
1-800-367-0111

ZOJIRUSHI HOME BAKERY BBCC-N15

Loaf Size: 1-Pound, 1½-Pound
Loaf Shape: Vertically Rectangular
Suggested Retail Price: $249.95

Cycles:

Preheat	**yes**	Dough/Manual	**yes**
(Warms cold ingredients before		Whole Wheat	**no**
mixing and during both Kneading		French Bread	**no**
cycles)		Raisin/Nut	**yes**
Rapid Bake	**no**	Jam/Rice	**no**
(But the Fresh Milk cycle bakes 1		Cake/Quick Bread	**yes**
hour Faster than the Dry Milk		Cool Down	**no**
cycle)			

Other Features:

Delayed Bake Timer	**yes**	Power Saver	**yes**
Viewing Window	**no**	*(20 Seconds)*	
Crust Color Selection	**no**		

Customer Service Phone Number:
1-800-733-6270

HINTS ON PRODUCING THE BEST LOAVES WITH THIS BREAD MACHINE:

• The Dry Milk setting bakes bread in 4 hours. The Fresh Milk setting bakes bread in 3 hours.

• Place the bread pan in the machine and wait 30 seconds before pressing the Start button. This allows the temperature sensor at the bottom of the pan adequate time to register cold ingredients.

• Make sure both the mixing blade and the bread pan are firmly seated before starting the machine.

ZOJIRUSHI HOME BAKERY BBCC-S15

Loaf Size: 1-Pound, 1½-Pound
Loaf Shape: Vertically Rectangular
Suggested Retail Price: $349.95

Cycles:

Preheat	yes	French Bread	yes
(Warms cold ingredients before		Raisin/Nut	yes
mixing and during both Kneading		Jam	yes
cycles)		Rice	no
Rapid Bake	yes	Cake/Quick Bread	yes
Dough/Manual	yes	Cool Down	yes
Whole Wheat	no		
(But you can program the			
machine for longer Kneading and			
Rising cycles)			

Other Features:

Delayed Bake Timer	yes	Crust Color Selection	yes
Viewing Window	yes	Power Saver	yes

Other: **The Homemade Menu allows you to program and save your own set of kneading, rising, and baking times.**
A removable tray in the bottom of the machine makes cleanup easier.

Customer Service Phone Number:
1-800-733-6270

HINTS ON PRODUCING THE BEST LOAVES WITH THIS BREAD MACHINE:

• Place the bread pan in the machine and wait 30 seconds before pressing the Start button. This allows the temperature sensor at the bottom of the pan adequate time to register cold ingredients.

• Make sure both the mixing blade and the bread pan are firmly seated before starting the machine.

✦✦✦ 2 ✦✦✦

Bread-baking Facts and Guidelines

The Science and Art of Baking Bread
✦✦✦

We think it would be useful to share a few facts about bread baking in general. For those of you who have never baked a loaf of bread by hand, we'd like to give you a better understanding of some of the elements involved in producing that "mini-miracle" each time you press the Start button. For those of you who are experienced bread bakers, we hope we've done our research well enough to surprise you with one or two new facts.

THE ESSENTIAL INGREDIENTS

• Gluten, the protein found mainly in wheat flour, gives bread its structure. The higher the gluten content, the higher and stronger the loaf will be.

• Yeast, a living organism, is activated when it comes in contact with warm liquids. It feeds on sugars and produces bubbles of carbon dioxide gas, which cause the bread to slowly rise.

• Flour contains gluten, starch, and enzymes that can convert the starch into sugar.

• Liquids activate the yeast and bind the dough.

• Salt moderates the yeast's activity and strengthens the gluten structure.

MIXING/KNEADING THE DOUGH

• As the dough is mixed and later kneaded, the tangled elastic strands of gluten in the flour begin to unfold and form a weblike structure. (If you take a well-kneaded piece of dough, roll it out very thin, and hold it up to the light, you can easily see the gluten structure.)

• At the same time malt enzymes, found in both wheat flour and barley, begin to break down the starch molecules in the flour(s) and turn them into sugars . . . food for the yeast.

• The amount and type of kneading largely determines the final texture of the bread. The more you knead the dough (up to a point), the finer the texture will be. As you knead, you break up the little pockets of air being incorporated into the dough. It's these air pockets between the strands of gluten that fill up with the carbon dioxide produced by the yeast. The smaller the air pockets, the finer the bread's texture.

• It is possible to "overknead" bread dough . . . usually by machine, rarely by hand. Its structure will break down, the gluten will lose its elasticity, and you'll be left with a useless, sticky blob of dough. If you stopped and restarted your machine several times after each kneading cycle, you'd risk this happening to your dough.

• When kneading dough by hand, always work in any extra flour a little at a time. Avoid adding large quantities of flour to your dough all at once; you'll end up with a very tough, dry, heavy loaf of bread.

• Well-kneaded dough is smooth and satiny and has a soft, pliable body to it. You should be able to knead it with one hand at that point.

RISING OF THE DOUGH

• Once the dough has been fully kneaded by hand, it is covered and set in a warm location to rise. The dough will eventually double in size.

- As the dough sits, the yeast cells feed on the available sugars, multiply, and produce carbon dioxide gas and alcohol. (That's the fermentation process in a nutshell.) The ever-increasing bubbles of carbon dioxide fill up the open spaces between the weblike strands of gluten, causing the dough to expand and rise.

- The optimum rising temperature is between 80° and 85°F.

- If a dough is "forced" to rise faster by subjecting it to higher temperatures, it will also produce more alcohol, giving the bread a sour taste and unpleasant smell.

- To warm the oven slightly for rising, turn the oven on "warm" for 1 minute, then turn it off, and place the covered dough in the oven to rise until doubled.

- After the first rising, the bread is punched down and usually allowed to rise a second time. Since the yeast organisms have multiplied greatly in number, the loaf will double in size again in about half the time it took to do so the first time.

- Punching down the dough (deflating it gently with your fist) redistributes the yeast and provides it with more oxygen and new food sources. It also forces out some of the excess carbon dioxide and alcohol.

- After the second rising, the dough is turned out onto a floured or lightly oiled countertop, then gently shaped (to avoid breaking gluten strands), placed into bread pans, covered, and left to rise one last time.

- When shaping the dough into braids, dinner rolls, pizza crusts, etc., it's easier to handle if you first place it on a lightly floured surface, cover it, and allow it to rest for 10 to 15 minutes. The elastic gluten strands in the dough will relax and it will be much easier to handle. If you've ever struggled with a pizza dough that kept shrinking up every time you tried to stretch it out to the edges of the pan, try letting the dough rest and relax before shaping it to fit the pan. As our friend Jana Cason explains, it's just too "excited"! Also, try to avoid overhandling or adding more flour to the dough at this point. Overhandling and excess flour result in a very inflexible dough and a heavy, tough bread.

- The maximum number of risings is four or five; after that the yeast's food supply is exhausted.

- Breads containing acidic ingredients such as buttermilk, yogurt, sour cream, and lemon juice will rise faster than breads without these ingredients.

- The more you load breads down with heavy ingredients such as fruits and nuts, the slower they will rise.

- Whole-grain bread doughs and other doughs low in gluten need longer kneading times and are slow risers.

• The dough should not expand to more than double its size during the last rise. That leaves a little growing room for the "oven spring"—the yeast's grand finale.

• If the shaped loaves are allowed to "over-rise" to their maximum expansion before baking, oven spring will not occur. Instead, the gas cells will burst, the gluten structure will give way, and the loaves will collapse.

• It's fairly easy to spot over-risen doughs. They are very light, puffy, and have very little body. Rather than bake them and have disappointing results, simply reshape, let rise (watch them carefully this time), and then bake.

BAKING

• There is a wide assortment of baking pans that can be used when baking breads in the oven. If you choose to use a glass or black steel pan, reduce the recommended oven temperature by 25°F to avoid overbrowning the bread. Black pans produce dark-crusted breads, silver pans produce light-crusted breads. If you bake free-form loaves, choose a sturdy stainless-steel baking sheet. There are also special curved French bread pans that will hold two loaves. They are perforated along the bottom to produce crisp crusts. Pizza and baking stones also produce very crisp crusts. Follow the manufacturer's instructions very carefully—they crack if not handled properly. We've read recipes for breads baked in coffee cans, flower pots, on quarry tiles, etc. We caution you to use containers specifically designed for food use to avoid contaminating your breads with toxic materials.

• When the bread is put into the hot oven, the heat causes one last surge in the yeast's activity. More carbon dioxide is created, the gas expands quickly, and there is a rapid increase in the loaf's size. This is called "oven spring."

• Once the interior of the bread reaches 140°F, the yeast dies and the leavening gasses and alcohol evaporate.

• A light-colored loaf will be less flavorful than a dark one.

• Brushing or spraying loaves with water during baking will produce a crisp crust. Loaves brushed with an egg wash before baking will have a shiny, golden crust. Milk brushed on a loaf prior to baking will give it a glossy, dark brown finish. For a soft, tender crust, brush the bread with butter or margarine right after removing it from the oven.

• A perfectly baked loaf of bread is golden brown, nicely rounded on top, hollow sounding when tapped on the bottom, and firm to the touch. It shouldn't be split around the edges, sunken in the middle, or oddly shaped. When the bread has been allowed to cool and then sliced, the interior should reveal a fine crumb with no large air tunnels. Each slice should have a firm body to it and the air pockets should be tiny and uniform in size. If the slice is coarse and full of large holes, very dry and crumbly, or limp, it will be difficult to butter or use in a sandwich.

• Remove bread from pan promptly after baking and place on a wire rack to cool.

• As tempting as that hot bread is, try to let it rest a minimum of 15 minutes before slicing; an hour is even better. It will set up and be much easier to slice. Some very soft breads need even longer—as much as overnight— before they're "sliceable."

Essential Guidelines for
Bread Machine Baking
❖❖❖

You will find some of these guidelines in your bread machine instruction booklet. The rest come from our personal experience as well as shared thoughts and suggestions from other bread machine bakers.

INGREDIENTS

• Breads turn out best when the ingredients are at room temperature, especially the liquids. (The very knowledgeable bakers at Red Star Yeast recommend an optimum liquid temperature of 80°F.) A quick 60 seconds on HIGH in the microwave will warm a cold cup of milk to about that temperature.

• Heavier breads such as the whole-grain loaves containing whole wheat, rye, oatmeal, etc., and breads containing a large quantity of extra ingredients such as raisins, nuts, seeds, grains, or cheese will not be as tall as simple white breads.

• Stay within the prescribed amounts of flour and liquids recommended for your machine. Trying to double a recipe could put an undue burden on your machine's motor and would definitely overflow the pan during baking.

• For best results, use only fresh ingredients.

• Any ingredients that were heated, roasted, or cooked should be cooled to room temperature before adding them to the rest of the ingredients in the bread pan.

• For whole-grain, cheese, or egg breads and loaves containing a high percentage of sugar or fat, select a Light Crust and/or Sweet Bread setting to avoid burnt crusts.

MEASURING INGREDIENTS

• It is very important to measure all ingredients carefully when using a bread machine. Sometimes as little as one tablespoon of liquid can make the difference between success and failure.

• To measure liquids properly, place the measuring cup on a level surface, pour in the liquid, then check the measurement at eye level.

• To measure flour properly, stir it first with a spoon to aerate it, then lightly spoon the flour into the measuring cup (do not press it in with the back of the spoon or tap the sides of the measuring cup to pack it down); level it with a straight-edged knife or spatula. Don't be a flour scooper! (We know you scoopers are out there . . . we meet you all the time. You're lovely people, but knock it off!) What happens when you dip into the bag or canister of flour with your measuring cup is that you pack in several extra tablespoons of flour each time. Two or three scoops and you have a great deal of extra flour you're not aware that you're adding. If your breads are consistently heavy, small, and dry, this is probably the reason why.

• If you can't resist packing ingredients into a measuring cup, save that urge for when you're measuring shortening and brown sugar. They should be firmly pressed down into the measuring cup.

JUDGING THE DOUGH

• This is a bread-baking skill worth developing. It will spare you many a ruined loaf. Experienced hands-on bread bakers develop a sixth sense for the proper "feel" of well-kneaded dough and the right ratio of liquid to dry ingredients. You'll learn to judge it with your eyes and ears and an occasional touch.

• When trying a recipe for the first time, it's always wise to check the dough several times during both kneading cycles and then later on at the end of the rising period. If your machine doesn't have a viewing window, be brave. Open the lid and peek in! We've run across many new owners who are afraid to open up the machine and look inside. We refer to this now as "The Jack-in-the-Box Syndrome."

• Most breads, by the end of the first mixing/kneading cycle, should form a ball of dough around the mixing blade. At this stage, the dough will usually be sticky to the touch and sometimes only partially mixed. There may also be traces of dough on the bottom or sides of the bread pan. By the end of the second kneading cycle, dough that is the proper consistency will form a definite silky, smooth ball with no film of dough still clinging to the sides or bottom of the pan. It will feel tacky when lightly touched. Whole-grain flours are slower to absorb moisture, so whole wheat and rye breads should be slightly wetter to the touch than white. (Yes, your own experience is the only way to determine the differences between "sticky," "tacky," and "slightly wetter to the touch.")

• We recommend following the recipe as written the first time you bake a bread, making no adjustments to the liquid or flour unless it's quite obvious that the dough is exceptionally dry or wet. We caution you about making changes to the recipe the first time because there are always those doughs that are exceptions to the rule. For instance, every time we make a banana bread, after the second kneading, the dough flattens out into a wet puddle and we're convinced it will never bake up properly. And every time, it bakes up into a spectacular loaf!

• If, after your first trial run, the bread was a disappointment, make note of how it turned out and refer to our troubleshooting chapter (page 109) for advice on how to correct it.

• Most problems occur when the dough is either too wet or too dry. Once you start observing the dough as it mixes, you'll soon develop an eye for the proper consistency at various stages during the kneading cycles.

• After several minutes of kneading, if the dough appears too wet, you can correct it by adding more flour, one tablespoon at a time, until it reaches the proper consistency. The same holds true if the dough appears very dry, crumbly, and won't hold together. Add extra liquid, one tablespoon at a time, until the dough forms a ball. We must add that unless the dough appears to be *extremely* wet or dry, we usually wait until the second kneading cycle to make any adjustments. Some doughs just take longer to absorb moisture than others.

• Remember: The desired end result is a silky smooth ball that is tacky to the touch. (When the kneading ends, the ball of dough will usually lose its round shape and settle in to fill up the corners of the pan.)

• If you make changes to the recipe, be sure to jot them down. Next time you make that bread, you can observe the bread just for fun! The hard part is behind you.

• In addition to eyeballing the appearance of the dough and touching it to judge its tackiness, another of your five senses should come into play: your sense of hearing. It's also important to listen to your machine as it goes about mixing and kneading the dough. In some cases, the dough may be too heavy or stiff and your machine will struggle to continue mixing it. It may even begin to stall. To alleviate the stress on your bread machine's motor, add more liquid, a tablespoon at a time, to soften the dough and facilitate kneading. Listen closely again. You may even detect a soft sigh from your machine and a whispered "thank you."

• The other time it's advantageous to take a quick peek at the dough is near the end of the final rising stage, shortly before it starts to bake. "Oven spring," which we described on page 42, also applies to the bread machine. Have you noticed how your bread takes a final jump in height during the first eight to ten minutes of baking? That's "oven spring." So if your dough is already nearing the lid of your machine at the end of the rising phase, you have a calamity about to take place. We've never heard of a bread strong enough to pop open the lid of the machine but we have witnessed many a loaf flow down the outside of the bread pan. If you catch it in time, a prick or two with a toothpick to deflate the top of the loaf will save you from a monumental cleanup job. (Flour and water baked onto the interior of your bread machine for an hour puts super glue to shame!)

THE WEATHER CAN AFFECT YOUR BREADS

• We'll discuss this in length later on, but if you're a new bread baker, you need to know from the beginning that the weather can sometimes play havoc with your loaves. (It's also comforting to have something other than "pilot error" to blame those duds on, once in a while.)

• If it is exceptionally humid, dry, cold, hot—any extreme in climatic conditions—you need to make adjustments when adding your ingredients. See the Helpful Hints chapter (page 109) for specific advice.

DELAYED BAKE TIMER

• Always keep the yeast dry when using the delayed timer setting. The moment the yeast combines with the liquids, it begins to activate. To prevent

it from activating prematurely, place all liquid ingredients in the bottom
bread pan, followed by the dry ingredients on top. Make a well in th
for the yeast. (Panasonic/National bread machines have a yeast dis
keeping the yeast separate is no problem.)

• Do not use any items on the delayed timer setting that would spoil
when left out of the refrigerator for several hours. Such items would include
milk, eggs, buttermilk, sour cream, and cottage cheese. Water plus powdered
substitutes can be used to replace the milk, eggs, and buttermilk in recipes
listing those ingredients.

Measurements/Conversions

1½ teaspoons = ½ tablespoon
3 teaspoons = 1 tablespoon
4 tablespoons = ¼ cup
5⅓ tablespoons = ⅓ cup
16 tablespoons = 1 cup

⅛ cup = 2 tablespoons
⅜ cup = ¼ cup + 2 tablespoons
⅝ cup = ½ cup + 2 tablespoons
⅞ cup = ¾ cup + 2 tablespoons
1⅛ cup = 1 cup + 2 tablespoons

2 tablespoons = ⅛ cup = 1 ounce
8 tablespoons = ½ cup = 4 ounces
16 tablespoons = 1 cup = 8 ounces = ½ pint
2 cups = 16 ounces = 1 pint = ½ quart
4 cups = 32 ounces = 2 pints = 1 quart
8 cups = 64 ounces = 4 pints = 2 quarts = ½ gallon
16 cups = 128 ounces = 8 pints = 4 quarts = 1 gallon

1 cup all-purpose flour = 130 grams = 4.59 ounces
1 cup bread flour = 135 grams = 4.76 ounces
1 cup whole wheat flour = 128 grams = 4.51 ounces

4 ounces grated cheese = 1 cup
1 stick of butter = 8 tablespoons = ½ cup = ¼ pound
1 pound of butter = 2 cups
1 large egg = scant ¼ cup liquid
1 lemon = 2 to 3 tablespoons juice
1 lemon = 4 teaspoons grated rind
1 medium orange = 6 to 8 tablespoons juice
1 medium orange = 2½ tablespoons grated rind

• To measure flour properly, stir it first with a spoon to aerate it, then lightly spoon the flour into a measuring cup (do not press it in with the back of the spoon or tap the sides of the measuring cup to pack it down); level it with a straight-edged knife or spatula. Do not scoop flour out of the bag or cannister with the measuring cup. You'll end up with an extra tablespoon or two of flour per cup, enough to make a big difference in your bread.

• Measure liquids by placing the measuring cup on a level surface, pour in the liquid, then check the measurement at eye level. A clear glass or plastic liquid measuring cup is essential. Do not use your dry measuring cup.

• Shortening and brown sugar should be firmly packed into the measuring cup before leveling off.

3

Ingredients

Wheat Flours
✦✦✦

The wheat berry consists of an outer layer (the bran), a small embryo inside (the germ) and the starchy interior (the endosperm), which provides food for the developing seed. Bread flour, which is the milled endosperm of hard winter and spring wheat kernels, has the highest gluten content among the white flours, and it produces the highest rising loaves. Spring wheat flour is planted in the spring and is harvested late summer; winter wheat is planted in the fall but lies dormant under winter snows and is later harvested in the early summer. Spring wheats are generally a little higher in gluten than winter wheats.

Whole wheat flour contains all elements of the wheat kernel: the germ, the bran, and the endosperm. For that reason, it also contains more nutrients, fiber, and natural oils. Whole wheat breads are denser and usually less tall than strictly white flour loaves.

Milling grains today usually involves grinding them between rapidly rotating steel cylinders until crushed, or smashing them with swiftly moving steel hammer heads, turning the grains to powder instantly. Both methods involve speed and high temperatures. Stone-ground flour, as the name suggests, is crushed between stone mills, but at a much slower pace and lower temperature than the more modern methods. The value of the "old-fashioned" stone milling process is that nutrients are not lost to the excessive heat and oxidation created by the more "efficient" methods.

White flour should be stored in airtight containers in a cool (75°F or less), dry location. If properly stored, the shelf life for commercial flour is 15 months from the coded date on the back of the package. (To decipher the date, simply call the 800 number listed on the package for directions.)

If you have a problem with weevils during the warm summer months, place newly purchased flour in the freezer for several days. Then store it in a tightly sealed container. You shouldn't have any further problems with "unwelcome guests."

Whole wheat and any other whole-grain flours should be kept under refrigeration to prevent the natural oils in the wheat germ and bran from turning rancid. If you choose to freeze them, know that freezing destroys vitamin E. (Note: If you plan to hand-mill your own grains, grind only enough flour for immediate use. Freshly ground flour will turn rancid rapidly and begin to lose valuable nutrients within two to three days. The raw grains, however, will keep indefinitely.)

ALL-PURPOSE FLOUR

• All-purpose flour is a blend of hard and soft wheats and was created to be a single flour that would work well in all recipes from delicate cakes to hearty breads.

• All-purpose flour is the milled starchy endosperm of the wheat kernel. The bran and wheat germ have been removed. Its natural yellowish tinge has been chemically whitened, usually with a chlorine gas.

• The average protein/gluten content is 10 to 11 percent.

• Breads baked in the bread machine using all-purpose bleached or unbleached flour will be significantly smaller than those made with bread flour with its higher amount of gluten.

UNBLEACHED FLOUR

• Unbleached flour is an all-purpose flour that has whitened with age; however, that aging process may have been chemically accelerated.

BREAD FLOUR

• Bread flour produces the highest loaves. You will find it in the market labeled "bread flour" or "Better for Bread Flour."

• Bread flour is also ground from the endosperm of the wheat kernel, but it is composed of strictly hard wheat flour, not a mixture of hard and soft wheat like all-purpose flour.

• The protein/gluten content of bread flour can be anywhere from 12 to 16 percent; usually, it's right around 14 percent.

• Gluten absorbs water; consequently, a bread-flour dough requires more liquid than a dough made from all-purpose flour.

• Some bread flours have potassium bromate added. It strengthens the gluten; higher loaves are a result. This is known as "bromated flour," which some bread machine manufacturers recommend. Other commercial bread flours contain ascorbic acid (vitamin C) instead of potassium bromate. It, too, aids in creating higher-rising loaves.

SELF-RISING FLOUR

• Baking soda and salt have been added to all-purpose flour to create self-rising flour. Self-rising flour is not recommended for use in bread machine recipes because it has less gluten than bread flour and a higher sodium content. It is best used in non-yeast baked goods.

CAKE/PASTRY FLOUR

• Again, these flours are obviously better suited for purposes other than bread baking. They are both milled from low-gluten, soft wheat.

INSTANT FLOUR

• This flour is also not appropriate for bread baking. It usually comes in a can and because of its quick-mixing properties, is best put to use thickening sauces and gravies.

WHOLE WHEAT FLOUR

• Whole wheat flour contains all three components of the wheat kernel: the bran, the germ, and the endosperm.

• Whole wheat breads will not be as tall as loaves made with bread flour. If your whole wheat breads are too small, replacing a portion of the whole wheat flour with bread flour or adding gluten will help. (You can purchase vital wheat gluten at most health food stores.)

• Usually, stone-ground wheat flour is coarser than the steel-ground whole wheat flour. The coarser the flour, the harder it is for the gluten to develop fully. As a result, breads made with stone-ground flour or coarsely ground hand-milled flour do not rise as high as other whole-grain flours. You will probably want to add gluten or some other dough enhancer and/or extra yeast.

• Whole-grain flours take longer to absorb moisture; the dough should feel more moist than a white-flour dough. If it is dry and stiff to the touch, that means it has too much flour, not enough liquid, and that it will result in a small, heavy, and very dense loaf. We all know them well—the infamous "doorstops" and "hockey pucks."

WHOLE WHEAT BREAD FLOUR

• Some health food stores sell this type of whole wheat flour. It is ground from hard wheat and has a higher gluten content than regular whole wheat flour.

• You can essentially create your own whole wheat bread flour by adding up to one tablespoon gluten to each cup of whole wheat flour.

WHITE WHOLE WHEAT FLOUR

• This is a fairly new flour on the market and not widely available as of this writing (see Sources, page 189). It's good news for those not particularly fond of the full-bodied, slightly bitter flavor of whole wheat. White whole wheat flour provides the same nutrients as whole wheat flour but has the mild, sweeter taste of white all-purpose flour.

• White whole wheat flour can be used in any recipe—even gravy—calling for all-purpose flour.

• Treat this flour as you would regular whole wheat flour; it still needs the longer kneading and rising times. The finished product resembles a loaf made with 50 percent all-purpose flour and 50 percent whole wheat flour.

WHOLE WHEAT PASTRY FLOUR

• Whole wheat pastry flour is ground from soft wheat, which means it has a low gluten content. It's comparable to cake flour and not suited for bread machine baking.

GRAHAM FLOUR

• Graham flour is soft winter wheat that resembles whole wheat flour in taste but has less protein (gluten). It will not produce as tall a loaf as regular whole wheat flour.

DURUM FLOUR

• Durum wheat, from which durum flour is ground, is the hardest of the wheats. A bread made entirely from durum wheat would be inedible.

SEMOLINA FLOUR

• Semolina flour is a refined durum flour, minus the bran and wheat germ. It is highly prized as a pasta flour. Combined with liquid and oil, it forms a very stiff dough, making possible a multitude of pasta shapes.

• Semolina flour can also be used in breads.

TRITICALE FLOUR

• Triticale is a hybrid grain—a cross between rye, durum, and red winter wheat.

• It is higher in protein than either wheat or rye flours but low in gluten. For a decent-size loaf, you need to combine it with at least an equal amount of high-gluten wheat flour.

• Triticale flour has a "ryelike" sweet, nutty flavor.

KAMUT FLOUR

• An ancient grain, kamut is a relative of durum wheat.

• It is high in protein and potassium and contains a unique type of gluten that is easier for the body to utilize than regular wheat.

• Kamut flour, though high in protein, is low in gluten. It must be combined with higher-gluten wheat flour to produce an acceptable bread.

SPELT FLOUR

• Spelt is an ancient wheat once grown in Mesopotamia that can survive very hostile growing conditions.

• Some people who are allergic to wheat find they can tolerate spelt wheat. Check with your allergist first to be sure.

• Spelt flour contains enough gluten to be an adequate substitute for wheat flours.

Non-wheat Flours
✦✦✦

Non-wheat flours contain very small amounts of gluten; consequently, they must be combined with wheat flours to produce a normal-size loaf. We found that using a 2½:1 ratio (2½ parts wheat flour to 1 part non-wheat flour) generally worked well.

Well-stocked grocery stores now carry the most common non-wheat flours such as rye and barley, but the best place to find all these flours under one roof is a health food store. If you're interested in experimenting with one or two of the more exotic flours and your health food store doesn't carry them, refer to the list of Sources (page 189).

LIGHT/MEDIUM RYE FLOUR

• This is a light grayish-tan flour ground from the endosperm of the rye grain. It does not contain the bran or germ.

• It produces breads with a hearty, old-world country flavor.

• Rye flour is high in protein but low in gluten. You need to use at least 2 cups of wheat flour for each cup of rye flour to produce an acceptable loaf in a bread machine.

DARK/PUMPERNICKEL RYE FLOUR

• Ground from the whole rye grain, it contains the bran and the germ as well as the endosperm.

• It has a coarser texture than light/medium rye flour and bakes up into a darker loaf.

• This flour is usually more difficult to locate. It's best suited for the dark pumpernickels and rustic black breads.

OAT FLOUR

• If you cannot locate oat flour in your health food store, try making your own. Place rolled oats in a blender or food processor and process until finely ground. You can also create oat flour by grinding whole oat groats in a hand mill.

• Oat flour contains an antioxidant, which acts as a preservative, helping the bread to retain its freshness longer.

• It is very high in protein, low in gluten, and must be combined with wheat flour to produce an acceptable loaf.

BARLEY FLOUR

• Barley flour has a mild sweet flavor and low gluten content, and is pale gray in color.

• Barley breads should contain at least 3 cups wheat flour for every 1 cup barley flour.

• It is perishable and should be stored in the refrigerator or freezer.

• Barley flour lends a soft, almost cakelike texture to breads and a subtle sweetness to the taste.

BUCKWHEAT FLOUR

• Made from grinding buckwheat groats, this flour is high in protein, relatively high in fat, and very low in gluten.

• It's a pungent, tart, earthy-tasting flour that lends a grayish color to the finished bread. It is best used in small amounts, no more than ½ cup per loaf.

MILLET FLOUR

• Millet flour is high in protein but very low in gluten.

• It is a light, yellowish flour with a slightly gritty texture.

• Breads baked with millet flour tend to be dry and crumbly in texture. We preferred using millet flour on a 3:1 ratio (3 parts wheat flour, 1 part millet flour).

AMARANTH FLOUR

• Amaranth is higher in protein, lysine, iron, and calcium than most other grains.

• Use this low-gluten flour in combination with high-gluten wheat flour; ½ cup amaranth flour per loaf will suffice.

TEFF FLOUR

• Teff flour has been favored by the highland Ethiopians for centuries.

• This light flour has a high ratio of bran and germ because the teff grain is the smallest of all grains.

• Combine teff flour with wheat flour for an acceptable-size loaf.

STORAGE

• Whole-grain flours that still contain some or all of the bran and germ should be stored in the refrigerator or freezer. These include dark rye, barley, buckwheat, millet, amaranth, and quinoa.

Gluten-free Flours and Grains
❖❖❖

Brown and/or white rice flours form the basis of most gluten-free breads. To vary the flavor, substitute other gluten-free flours and grains in ¼-, ½-, or 1-cup quantities. The possible combinations are limited only by your imagination! For instance, we replaced 1 cup of rice flour with 1 cup of corn flour and produced a mild-flavored, great change-of-pace bread.

RICE FLOUR

• Both brown and white rice flours are available. Brown rice flour includes the rice bran and, therefore, is more nutritious and has more fat than white rice flour.

• Bread made with rice flour instead of wheat flour has a sweet flavor and chewy texture.

• Rice flour is the most common substitute for wheat flour when baking gluten-free breads.

SWEET RICE FLOUR

• This is a waxy form of rice flour that is not normally used in baked goods. It's better suited for thickening sauces.

POTATO STARCH FLOUR

• This is the finely milled starch from the potato. It helps retain the bread's moisture and freshness and aids in the fermentation of the yeast.

POTATO FLOUR

• Unlike potato starch flour, this heavy flour is made from cooked potatoes that have been dried and then ground into flour. It gives a definite potato taste to breads.

• To avoid lumping, blend it with the sugar and fat before adding liquids.

SOY FLOUR

• Soy flour is high in protein (amino acids), iron, and calcium.

• It has a rather bitter, bean-like flavor that some find objectionable. It should be used sparingly; start with two tablespoons per loaf and increase the amount in future loaves as your taste buds dictate.

• Breads made with soy flour will be moist and finely textured.

• There are both regular and low-fat soy bean flours. If using the regular flour, make sure it is fresh. Store it in the refrigerator or freezer to prevent it from going rancid.

TAPIOCA FLOUR

• Tapioca flour is processed from the roots of the cassava plant.

CORN FLOUR

• A low-protein flour with a sweet flavor.

• Yellow or white corn can be milled into a fine flour.

QUINOA FLOUR

• Quinoa flour is very high in protein and has a nutty taste.

• This ancient flour is very similar to amaranth flour in nutrition and history.

• It can also be used to make gluten-free pasta.

LEGUME FLOURS

• These gluten-free flours include pea, mung, lentil, soy, and garbanzo bean flours.

• Created by grinding various beans, they add their own unique personality to breads.

CORNMEAL

• Cornmeal is coarsely ground yellow, white, or blue corn.

• Add ½ cup of cornmeal to gluten-free breads and it will give the loaf a crumbly texture and sweet taste.

• Store freshly milled cornmeal in the refrigerator for two to three weeks at the most.

QUINOA

• This tiny grain should be rinsed well before using to remove any traces of its bitter coating.

• Add up to ½ cup whole quinoa to gluten-free breads for a sweet, nutty taste.

STORAGE

• Store corn flour, brown rice flour, soy flour, and cornmeal in the refrigerator or freezer to prevent rancidity.

Whole Grains

These are all the wonderful "extras" that add so much flavor, texture, and wholesome goodness to whole-grain breads. They can be cooked, toasted, soaked, or sprouted and then added to your bread. Some, like rolled oats and cornmeal, can be used as is. (If rolled grains, meals, flakes, or cereals are added to the mix dry, they will soak up moisture from the dough, causing it to be a dry or crumbly bread. Be sure to add extra liquid when adding dry, uncooked grains to your dough.)

You can add as little as 1 tablespoon of whole grains per cup of flour or as much as ¼ cup whole grains per cup of flour to your breads; your taste buds and the bread's density and texture should be your guide. The more grains you add, the heavier, denser, and more crumbly the bread will be. It will also be more nutritious. Whole grains can simply be added to your favorite bread; no need to delete a like amount of flour. Watch the dough as it kneads and add more liquid or flour if necessary.

As a general rule of thumb, whole grains such as wheat berries, kamut, whole oats, and triticale should be soaked in water overnight, then simmered on the stovetop in a covered saucepan for 30 to 60 minutes, until they are tender. Drain them well in a colander. Rice, barley, rye, amaranth, quinoa, buckwheat groats (kasha), millet, teff, and cracked wheat do not require soaking to soften them before being cooked. Remember to let the grains cool before adding them to your bread dough in quantities up to ¼ cup whole grain per cup of flour.

To sprout whole grains: rinse them first, then cover them with warm water and let stand at room temperature for approximately 15 hours. Drain off the water and rinse the berries in fresh water. Place them in a clean glass jar, cover the top with a damp piece of cheese cloth, and secure it with a rubber band. Set the jar on its side and place it in a warm, dark spot. Rinse

the berries with fresh water every 12 hours until they begin to sprout (no need to remove the cheese cloth each time). At this point they are ready to be used in a recipe. The whole process should take two to three days. Use approximately ¼ cup sprouted berries per cup of flour. Be sure to drain them well first.

You can toast grains such as oats, millet, amaranth, and quinoa in a skillet over medium heat or in a baking pan, in a 300°F oven for ten to fifteen minutes. Watch closely to avoid scorching them.

WHOLE WHEAT BERRIES

• You should be able to find red winter or spring wheat kernels in your local health food store. They're teeth crunchers if you attempt to eat them raw, but if you sprout them first, they'll be much more edible (and less hazardous). Sprouted wheat will add a surprising sweet taste and moistness to your breads.

• They can also be cooked and added to the bread dough. To cook, soak whole wheat berries overnight in water, then drain them and add 1 cup of the soaked kernels to 3½ cups boiling water. Bring the water back to a boil, cover the saucepan with a lid, reduce the heat to low, and simmer for 50 to 60 minutes until tender.

• Well-drained cooked or sprouted wheat berries can be added to your breads in quantities up to ¼ cup berries per cup of flour.

• If you are interested in milling your own flours, we've found that 1 cup of whole wheat kernels produces approximately 1¾ cups of medium-ground whole wheat flour.

WHEAT BRAN

• The bran is the outer hull of the wheat kernel. It does contain some fat.

• Wheat bran is usually sold as "miller's bran" or "unprocessed bran flakes" in grocery and health food stores.

• Bran adds fiber, texture, and flavor to homemade breads.

• Limit the amount of wheat bran used in recipes to ¼ cup per cup of flour. The sharp edges of the bran cut the gluten strands and thereby reduce the bread's elasticity.

• You can either add bran to a favorite recipe (plus some additional liquid) or replace part of the flour with bran (which will produce a heavier, smaller loaf).

• Store bran in a cool, dry place up to one month, three months in the refrigerator, or up to one year in the freezer.

WHEAT GERM

• The germ is the embryo of the wheat kernel. Added to breads, it increases its nutritional value and adds a nutty flavor.

• In large quantities, wheat germ will inhibit the gluten's growth. Use no more than 2 tablespoons in the larger 1½-pound loaves or 1½ tablespoons in 1-pound loaves. It isn't necessary to reduce the amount of flour when adding wheat germ to a recipe.

• Wheat germ contains a great deal of natural oil. To prevent rancidity, store it in the refrigerator or in the freezer; however, freezing will destroy the germ's vitamin E.

CRACKED WHEAT

• These are whole wheat berries that have been broken into rather large pieces. Again, they are too hard to eat as is; they need to be softened first by cooking them. To cook, add 1 cup cracked wheat to 2⅓ cups boiling water, return water to a boil, stir, cover, and simmer on low heat for 15 minutes.

• As a rule, add no more than ¼ cup well-drained, cooked cracked wheat per cup of flour to a favorite bread.

BULGUR

• Bulgur is cracked wheat that has also been parboiled; consequently, it will absorb liquids faster than cracked wheat. Uncooked and added to bread doughs it will give a flavorful, crunchy texture to your breads.

• To soften it, soak 1 cup bulgur in 2 cups boiling water for one half hour, then drain and cool.

• As with cooked cracked wheat, drain bulgur well and add a maximum of ¼ cup bulgur per cup of flour to any recipe for additional fiber and nutrients.

WHOLE WHEAT FLAKES

• These flakes of wheat resemble rolled oats. They're created by heating and pressing whole wheat berries.

• You may have passed them by without ever noticing them. Check the bulk bins or the packaged grains more closely next time you visit your local health food store.

• Experiment by substituting whole wheat flakes for wheat bran or oatmeal in a recipe.

WHOLE RYE BERRIES

• As the wheat berry is to whole wheat flour, the rye berry is to dark rye flour. These kernels can be sprouted and then added to any of your rye breads for extra flavor in quantities up to ¼ cup sprouted berries per cup of flour. They are an additional ingredient, not a substitution for flour.

• Rye berries can also be ground into a dark rye flour.

• To cook whole rye berries, place 1 cup of the grain into 3 cups of boiling water. Return the water to a boil, cover, reduce the heat, and simmer for 1 hour.

CRACKED WHOLE RYE

• On the off chance that you might be able to locate this grain, treat it much the same as cracked wheat. It needs to be cooked before it is added to bread doughs. To 3½ cups boiling water, add 1 cup cracked whole rye. Return to a boil, cover the pot, and allow to simmer for 30 minutes.

• Cooked and well-drained, cracked whole rye can be added to your favorite rye breads in ¼-cup-per-cup-of-flour quantities. A like amount of flour does not need to be omitted from the recipe.

WHOLE RYE FLAKES

• If you were lucky enough to find cracked whole rye, set your sights for whole rye flakes next. Just like wheat and rolled oat flakes, they're whole rye berries that have been heated and pressed flat.

• Substitute rye flakes in recipes calling for rolled oats for a change of flavor.

ROLLED OATS

• The inedible husk that surrounds the oat kernel is removed; the grain is then sliced, steamed, rolled, and dried to produce rolled oats.

• Quick-cooking oats are rolled flatter and heat treated longer than regular oats, making them faster cooking.

• We recommend old-fashioned rolled oats, not the quick-cooking variety in bread recipes. We think they hold up better.

• Oats add a sweet, nutty, taste and chewy texture to bread. To intensify that flavor, you can toast them first.

• Breads containing oats stay fresher longer due to the natural antioxidant found in the oat's endosperm.

• For a change of pace, try adding up to 1 cup cooked oatmeal to your bread dough. You can use it as a replacement for the oats in an oatmeal bread or as an additional ingredient in a bread of your choice. (Don't forget to decrease the liquid in your recipe to allow for the moisture in the oatmeal.)

OAT GROATS

• Akin to wheat berries and whole rye berries, oat groats are the raw oat kernels with the outer hull removed. Like wheat and rye berries, they need to be soaked overnight and then cooked to make them edible.

• To cook, place 1 cup of oat groats (that have soaked overnight) in 3 cups boiling water, return to a boil, cover the pan, reduce the heat to low, and simmer the groats for 30 minutes.

• Like wheat berries, add up to ¼ cup cooked and drained oat groats per cup of flour in any recipe you choose. You won't need to reduce the flour by the equivalent amount; however, you may need to adjust the liquid/flour balance in your dough while it kneads.

STEEL-CUT OATS

• As their name suggests, these oat kernels have been thinly sliced with sharp steel blades, then heat-processed.

• This firm-textured cooked cereal is also known as Scottish oatmeal.

• Cook steel-cut oats, uncovered, in boiling water as you would rolled oats until they begin to thicken (15 minutes); cool, then add to breads in quantities up to 1 cup per loaf.

• You can use cooked oats as a replacement for rolled oats in an oatmeal bread (reduce the liquid in your recipe accordingly) or as an additional ingredient in other breads.

OAT BRAN

• Because of its blood cholesterol–lowering properties, oat bran is a very popular addition to homemade bread.

• Oat bran contains twice the soluble fiber of rolled oats.

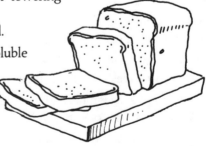

• Use oat bran sparingly in bread doughs—¼ cup oat bran per cup of flour. Just as wheat bran does, oat bran detracts from the gluten's structure and elasticity.

• You can add bran to a favorite recipe (plus some additional liquid) or replace part of the flour with bran (which will produce a heavier, smaller loaf).

BARLEY

• Pearled barley has had the outer hull removed and much of the bran and germ.

• Whole, hull-less barley contains the bran and germ; only the inedible outer hull has been removed.

• To cook barley, rinse it well, add 1 cup of the grain to 3½ cups boiling water, return the water to a boil, then cover, reduce the heat to low, and simmer for 30 to 35 minutes.

• Use hull-less barley rather than pearled barley for sprouting.

• When you include sprouted barley in your bread, it adds a wonderful, sweet flavor. Add as much as ¼ cup well-drained, sprouted barley per cup of flour.

• Sprouted barley can also be dried and ground to create diastatic malt powder, which is a natural dough enhancer and sugar substitute. It converts the flour's starch into sugar.

CORNMEAL

• Cornmeal is coarsely ground yellow, white, or blue corn.

• Added to bread, it will give it a crumbly texture and a sweet taste. It also weakens the gluten's strength, so ⅓ cup in a three-cup flour recipe is the maximum.

• Cornmeal that is "degerminated" has had the germ removed. Water-ground or stone-ground cornmeal still contains the germ.

• Cornmeal is very sweet tasting when freshly ground. If it has a strong, bitter smell and taste, it is stale.

• Store freshly milled cornmeal in the refrigerator for two to three weeks at most.

BUCKWHEAT GROATS (KASHA)

• Buckwheat is not a grain; it's actually a member of the rhubarb family.

• Add as much as ¼ cup of this pungent kernel to your breads in its cooked form (kasha) for each cup of flour in the recipe. It should be used as an additional ingredient rather than a flour substitute. You may need to reduce the liquid in the recipe or add an extra tablespoon or more of flour while the dough is kneading if it appears too wet.

MILLET

• Millet is a tiny, yellow, round grain with a mild flavor. It's high in protein and easily digested.

• You can add it as is to bread to give your loaves an interesting new texture and some extra crunch in each bite.

TRITICALE

• This whole grain is a cross between hard red wheat, durum wheat, and rye. It's the very first man-made grain.

• It can be sprouted, cooked, or ground into flour just like other whole grains.

• To cook triticale, first soak 1 cup of berries in water overnight. Next day, add the drained berries to 3 cups boiling water, return the water to a boil, cover, reduce the heat to low, and simmer for 60 to 70 minutes.

• Add well-drained, sprouted or cooked triticale berries to your breads for extra nutrition in quantities of up to ¼ cup berries per cup of flour.

AMARANTH

• This ancient grain's history dates back to the Aztecs in Mexico and Central America.

• Amaranth is not a grass like most other grains; it's a leaf plant belonging to the spinach family.

• This tiny, high-protein grain looks like cream-colored poppy seeds. It will add a sweet, nutty flavor to your breads.

• This extra ingredient for your breads can be added in quantities up to ¼ cup grain per cup of flour. It is not a flour substitute.

QUINOA

• Similar to amaranth, this ancient grain was a staple in years past for the Inca civilization.

• It is also nutritionally very similar to amaranth.

• Rinse this grain well before using to remove any traces of its bitter coating. (Dry it well, too, if you plan to grind it into flour.)

• Add as much as ¼ cup quinoa per cup of flour to your breads. You do not need to decrease the flour in the recipe by an equal amount.

KAMUT

• The kamut kernel has a buttery taste and is three times larger than a grain of wheat.

• It is a relative of durum wheat and should be cooked and cooled before adding it to your breads. To cook kamut, first soak 1 cup of the kernels in water overnight. The following day, add the drained kamut to 3 cups boiling water. Bring the water back to a boil, cover, reduce the heat, and simmer the grain for 30 to 40 minutes until tender.

• Once cooled and well drained, add at most only ¼ cup kamut for every cup of flour in the recipe. It should be used as an additional ingredient, not a flour substitute.

SORGHUM

• This milletlike grain can be used whole or ground into a sweet meal or flour for your breads.

Yeast

Yeast is a living organism, a single-cell plant. One pound of active dry yeast contains more than 3 billion of those yeast cells! There are about 160 known species of yeast but the one we're concerned with is the *saccharomyces cerevisiae* species. Different strains of it are used for active dry, compressed, fast-rising, and instant yeast. It's the same species of yeast used in brewing beer and wine; that's why it was also called "brewer's yeast" (not to be confused with the nutritional yeast of the same name that has no leavening properties because the yeast cells are dead). Active yeast organisms are found in high concentrations in the foam of newly made beer and wine. Initially, before the convenient little packets of active dry yeast came into being, bread bakers had to obtain their yeast from the local brewery. Imagine having to visit the local brewery/winery to bring home a cup of foam every time you felt like baking bread in your machine!

Since we now live in a more modern world, instead of begging a cup of foam from your local brewmeister, we recommend that you buy your yeast in 1-pound or 2-pound bulk packages at warehouse discount clubs, restaurant supply stores, or from bulk bins in health food stores. Initially, you'll look at that huge package of yeast and feel certain that you could never use it up in your lifetime. Trust us . . . you will! If you're still timid about buying that much yeast, or don't have easy access to a supplier, most markets now carry the convenient 4-ounce glass jars of active dry yeast.

As you'll notice in our recipes, we're partial to Red Star yeast. We stumbled on their product quite by accident and, because of what we found to be superior results, we've used and recommended it ever since. It is easily obtainable and reasonably priced, especially when bought in bulk. We've turned to the experts at Red Star many times for sound bread-baking advice. They're extremely busy people and we don't want to encourage anyone just to call and chitchat, but if you ever have yeast-related questions, you'll find everyone there very pleasant and helpful. Red Star's number is listed in the back of this book in the Sources section under Universal Foods Corporation (page 189).

THE FERMENTATION PROCESS

• Yeast is activated when it comes in contact with a warm liquid. To grow, it needs food (sugars), warmth, a slightly acidic environment, and some oxygen.

• The fermentation process begins with the yeast's consumption of available sugars. The first sugars it takes in are glucose, fructose, and the combination of the two: sucrose (table sugar). When those initial sugar supplies are depleted, it then feeds on maltose, the sugar created when the malt enzymes present in the dough convert some of the flour's starch into sugar.

• If you have the "If-some-is-good, more-is-better" outlook on life, it won't play out well when adding sugar to bread dough. True, some added sugar will help stimulate the yeast's growth, but large quantities will actually have the opposite effect.

• As the yeast feeds, it multiplies, and gives off two by-products: carbon dioxide and alcohol. Though the alcohol gives bread its wonderful aroma and flavor, if the dough is left too long to ferment (rise), the alcohol will eventually kill the yeast and produce a very bitter-tasting bread. Punching the dough down releases carbon dioxide gasses and allows some of the accumulated alcohol to evaporate.

• Yeast dough rises best at temperatures between 80° and 85°F.

• Salt is a necessary inhibitor of yeast's growth and also helps to strengthen the gluten's structure. If you omit the salt in recipes, it's most likely that your loaves will "overproof"—rise up very high then collapse when the heat is turned on.

• Salt, in high concentration, can also kill the yeast if the two come in contact as you're adding ingredients to the bread pan. Take care to keep them separated.

• Yeast doesn't respond well when it's doused with oil prior to mixing. So be good to your yeast. Add the oil to the liquids in the bottom of the pan, then the dry ingredients, and the yeast last.

ACTIVE DRY YEAST

• One ¼-ounce packet of yeast equals 2¼ teaspoons of yeast.

• Active dry yeast is available in strips of three ¼-ounce packets, 4-ounce jars, and 2-pound bulk packages.

• When using active dry yeast in a recipe made without a bread machine, the ideal liquid temperature is between 105° and 115°F. Testing at Red Star, however, has shown that a lower liquid temperature of 80°F yields the best results when baking breads in a bread machine. If you don't have a thermometer, 80°F water is in the "warm" range—not "cold," not "hot," but basically room temperature.

FAST-ACTING YEASTS

• Rapid-Rise, Quick-Rise, and Instant are all fast-acting yeasts. They cut the bread's rising time almost in half, but are also the James Deans of the yeast family; they live fast, give a stellar performance, but die young. For this reason, fast-acting yeasts are not well suited for multiple risings, long periods of fermentation (French breads, sourdoughs), or the long whole-wheat cycle on some bread machines.

• Fast-acting yeasts are available in strips of three ¼-ounce packets, 4-ounce jars, and 1-pound bulk packages.

• Fast-acting yeasts can be used in both the bread machine's Regular and Rapid Bake cycles. Use ½ teaspoon fast-acting yeast per cup of flour in the Regular cycle. When testing the fast-acting yeasts in the Rapid Bake cycle, we had much better results when we doubled the amount of yeast (1 teaspoon per cup of flour). We did find, however, that fast-acting yeast did not work as well as regular active dry yeast on either cycle in some machines.

• If your bread rises up beautifully but collapses once baking begins, try reducing the amount of fast-acting yeast in that particular recipe next time. (For other remedies, see our suggestions in the Helpful Hints section beginning on page 109.)

• Instant active dry yeast is very similar to rapid/quick-rise yeasts and can be used interchangeably with it. Use ½ teaspoon instant yeast per cup of flour in the Regular cycle; double that amount for the Rapid Bake cycle.

COMPRESSED (FRESH) YEAST

• Compressed yeast is sold in ⅗-ounce cakes and can usually be found in the deli cases of most markets. It must be kept refrigerated (up to two weeks) or frozen (up to two months). Once thawed, fresh yeast should be used right away.

• One ⅗-ounce cake of compressed yeast equals one ¼-ounce packet of active dry yeast.

• When fresh, it is light tan in color. If it has gone past its prime, it will turn brown.

• Compressed yeast should be dissolved in liquids no warmer than 95°F. Temperatures approaching 120°F will kill it.

• Most professional bakers use compressed yeast rather than active dry yeast. They prefer its lower activating temperature and find it more dependable to work with. Its very limited shelf life is no problem for them.

• Compressed yeast is not recommended by any bread machine manufacturers, but in our tests we found that it produced nicely shaped loaves that were, on average, one inch smaller than those made with active dry yeast. The disadvantage to the cake yeast is that its shelf life is approximately two weeks (or two months if frozen), making it very inconvenient. It's also more expensive to use.

HOW TO DETERMINE IF YOUR YEAST IS STILL ACTIVE

• In a 1-cup glass measuring cup, dissolve 1 teaspoon sugar in ½ cup warm water (110° to 115°F). Sprinkle 1 scant tablespoon yeast slowly over the surface. Stir; allow the mixture to sit for 10 minutes. Within the first 5 minutes, the yeast should begin rising to the surface. At the end of 10 minutes' time, if the yeast has doubled and reached the 1 cup mark and has a rounded crown of foam, it is very active. Yeast that is inactive or losing its potency will either not react at all or will not reach the 1-cup mark within 10 minutes. In either case, discard that package of yeast and buy a new one.

• If your breads suddenly bake up very small and dense, try testing your yeast before continuing.

• If you buy your yeast in bulk bins at health food stores, we recommend you test it before using it.

STORAGE

• Yeast deteriorates when it is exposed to heat, moisture, and oxygen.

• Active-dry and fast-acting yeasts should be kept in a cool, dry location. You can store the 3-strip packets at room temperature (use before the expiration date stamped on the package) or you can store the packets and the 4-ounce jars of yeast in the refrigerator.

• If you purchase the yeast in 1- or 2-pound bulk packages, remove a small quantity and store it in an airtight glass jar in the refrigerator. The remainder of the yeast should be well-wrapped, placed in a plastic bag, and stored in the freezer. Replenish your small jar of yeast with the frozen yeast as needed. Though the bulk package is not stamped with an expiration date, if you store it in the freezer, you will find that you'll use it up long before the yeast loses its potency. The bulk package will keep in the freezer at least one year. (By the way, Red Star bulk yeast is vacuum packed. We've known people who were hesitant to purchase it because it felt like a solid brick of yeast. They thought they'd have difficulty breaking off chunks and measuring it. Actually, when you open the package, that "brick of yeast" turns granular instantly. It never ceases to amaze and delight us. Sometimes it's even the high point of our day!)

• **One caution:** If you store your yeast in the refrigerator or freezer, do not zap it in the microwave to bring it to room temperature quickly. Like any living organism, yeast doesn't take kindly to microwaving.

Liquids
—✦✦✦—

The liquids bind all the ingredients together in a bread dough as well as activate the yeast's performance. There is a large selection of liquids to bake with and each will affect your bread in different ways.

WATER

• Breads using water as the only liquid have a crisper crust.

• The acidity or alkalinity of your tap water can have a dramatic effect on your breads. Very soft (acidic) water results in soft and sticky bread doughs due to poorly developed gluten. On the other hand, very hard (alkaline) water retards the yeast's fermentation. The happy medium for your bread dough is tap water with a slightly acidic pH balance.

• If you wish to determine the pH balance of your water, call your local water authority or health department. A pH of 7 is neutral. A pH from 5.5 to 6.5 would be perfect. (To give you the broader picture: orange juice has an acidic pH of 3.0, distilled water has an acidic pH of 5.5, milk has a 6.9 pH. On the other side of the scale, baking soda mixed in water has an alkaline 8.4 pH.)

• Once you determine your water's pH balance, you can counteract very hard water by adding about 1 to 1½ teaspoons lemon juice or vinegar to the tap water in your recipe. If you have very soft water, adding ¼ teaspoon baking soda to your recipe or replacing 2 tablespoons of your water with an egg white should return your bread dough to its most yeast-friendly state. In either case, a third option is to use a good-quality bottled water.

• Do not use softened water; it has a very high sodium content.

MILK

• Using milk as the liquid results in a bread with a golden brown color and a softer crust than those baked with water. It also adds a softer, finer texture and gives each slice its creamy white color.

• All milks can be used interchangeably with each other in bread recipes. By replacing whole milk with skim, all you "sacrifice" is fat.

• Certified raw milk contains certain enzymes that will interfere with the yeast's action. Scalding it first will destroy those enzymes.

NONFAT DRY MILK

• You can replace fresh milk in any recipe with water and several tablespoons nonfat dry milk powder. We generally use about 3 tablespoons powdered milk per cup of water. (Add the milk powder with the rest of the dry ingredients and keep it from mixing with the water if you plan to use the delayed-bake timer.)

• Store unopened powdered milk in a cool, dry place and don't keep it longer than a year. If your kitchen is quite warm, use it within a few months. It will eventually go bad and develop a strong, undesirable taste.

• Once opened, it is best to store nonfat dry milk in a tightly sealed container in the refrigerator, where it will remain fresh for a few months. It can also be stored at room temperature but doesn't fare well in humid weather.

• Lois buys her nonfat dry milk in bulk at a health food store. Linda buys the box of powdered milk that contains ten quart-size, sealed envelopes at the grocery store.

BUTTERMILK

• Most buttermilk is made with lowfat or skim milk that is first heated then cooled to room temperature. Next are added cultured bacteria that convert some of the milk sugar (lactose) into lactic acid. This gives buttermilk its distinctive thickness and tangy taste.

• It's the lactic acid that gives buttermilk breads a very tender crumb. Lactic acid also discourages bacterial growth, making it possible to keep buttermilk on hand longer than regular milk.

• You can create an acceptable substitute by adding 1 tablespoon distilled white vinegar or lemon juice to warm skim or low-fat milk. Stir and allow it to stand for five minutes.

• Buttermilk seems to vary considerably from brand to brand in flavor, acidity, and consistency. Once you find a brand you like, make a note of it.

• You just opened a quart of buttermilk to use 1⅛ cups in a buttermilk bread recipe. Now what? Well, if there are no buttermilk guzzlers in your family, our suggestion is to measure out 1⅛-cup quantities into separate, small containers and pop them into the freezer. Then you'll have buttermilk on hand when you decide to bake that bread again.

• Buttermilk will separate when frozen, so when you need it, thaw, and then shake vigorously before using.

POWDERED BUTTERMILK

• Powdered buttermilk is the perfect solution for those of you who don't have room in your freezer for cartons of buttermilk and use it only occasionally in breads.

• Use it just as you would nonfat dry milk powder; add 3 to 4 tablespoons powder per cup of water to the dry ingredients.

• Some very clever bread bakers on the Prodigy network noticed a significant difference in a particular bread baked with fresh buttermilk and the same bread baked with buttermilk powder. Several tests done with litmus strips proved their initial hunch to be correct: fresh buttermilk has a higher acid content than powdered. The recipe called for baking soda. That was okay in combination with the more acidic fresh buttermilk but it neutralized any beneficial effects the less-acidic powdered buttermilk might have had. The bottom line is, if you chose to use powdered buttermilk and the recipe also calls for baking soda, omit the baking soda.

OTHER LIQUIDS

• You can recapture some of those "lost" nutrients from the water in which you cooked vegetables or beans by using it as all, or part of, the liquid in your next bread. (If you plan to do this, avoid salting your vegetables or beans until you have removed them from the cooking water.)

• The water in which you boiled potatoes is another useful liquid. You will receive several added benefits: extra nutrients, a boost for the yeast, richer flavor, softer texture, and breads that stay fresh longer. So save that water!

• Speaking of vegetables, many of them contain a high degree of water (the same goes for fruits). If you toss in "a little of this and a little of that" (leftover veggies from dinner or the fruit your children bypassed at breakfast), the bread you're about to make may surprise you when it turns into one big gooey puddle in the bottom of your bread pan. When adding extra fruits or vegetables, the best place to start is by calculating half their measure to be water. In other words, if you were to add 1 cup chopped apples or 1 cup chopped onion to a bread recipe, assume that you're adding ½ cup water, also. Reduce the liquid in the recipe by ½ cup. Observe the dough as it mixes. If it appears too dry, you can add liquid one tablespoon at a time to correct it.

• Beer can be used as a liquid; it seems to match up best with whole wheat or whole-grain breads. For the most flavor, use dark, heavy beers. It helps to pour some in a cup, leave it out overnight, and let it go flat before trying to measure it.

Fats
—◆◆◆—

• Fats—butter, margarine, shortening, oil—add tenderness and flavor to breads, and keep the loaves from turning stale rapidly. (By coating the starch granules, fats slow down the moisture loss that causes staling.)

• Fats also contribute to the gluten's elasticity, making for higher rising loaves. As with sugar, however, too much added fat will have just the opposite effect on the gluten and result in a very heavy, compact loaf.

• You may use just about any of the fats interchangeably, but highly flavorful oils such as olive oil, sesame oil, etc., may throw off the flavor of sweet, delicate breads.

• If you use butter, unsalted sweet butter is normally fresher than salted butter. Salt is a preservative, so salted butter is often older. Unsalted butter spoils faster; store it in the freezer.

• If the recipe calls for more than 2 tablespoons of butter, cut it into several chunks, to facilitate mixing.

• We discuss fat substitutes in the next section. For those watching their fat intake (and who isn't these days), you'll be happy to know that most breads can be successfully baked with little or no fat.

Salt
—✧✧✧—

• Some salt is necessary when baking bread. Salt serves as a yeast inhibitor. It "chaperones" the multiplying yeast cells, keeping their activity in check and preventing "overproofing."

• Salt prevents excess acidity in the dough, contributes to a browner crust, and prevents the growth of unwanted bacteria. It also inhibits the activity of the protein-destroying enzymes in the flour that weaken the gluten's structure.

• Without salt, one of two things would happen: Your bread would rise up very tall and then collapse during baking, or your bread would never have the proper gluten strength to rise at all. Omitting the salt from a recipe is therefore not recommended. You can, however, usually reduce the amount of salt in the recipes with no problem.

• You can also use certain salt substitutes, which we discuss in the next chapter.

• Salt enhances the flavor of all the ingredients in your bread. Without it, your oddly shaped bread would also be very flat tasting.

• Regular table salt, sea salt, and coarse kosher salt all work well in bread machine recipes.

• If you use coarse salt, increase the recipe amount by approximately 1 teaspoon to allow for its coarser texture. Add it directly to the liquids to help it dissolve completely.

• DO NOT use rock salt as a substitute for coarse kosher salt. It is not meant for human consumption.

• When adding ingredients to the bread pan, keep the salt and the yeast separated. Concentrated amounts of salt are harmful to yeast.

Sweeteners
—✧✧✧—

Sugar's role in the bread-baking process is to provide food for the ravenous yeast cells. Most or all of that food can be obtained from the flour. Powerful malt enzymes break down starch granules and convert them into maltose (malt sugar). Adding extra sugar, in moderate amounts, will increase the yeast's fermentation activity by providing additional, readily accessible food for the yeast. But a heavy hand with the sugar spoon will have a negative effect on both the yeast and the gluten. Sugar attracts water and when too much is used, it robs the yeast and gluten of needed moisture.

Sugar makes breads more moist and tender, gives the crust a lovely golden color, and, because of its moisture-attracting properties, also helps delay the staling process, which dries out bread.

There is a huge variety of sugars and each of them can add a different personality to your breads. You can often replace one sugar for another to vary the bread's flavor, but not always measure for measure. We have calculated some of those variations for you. If you substitute a "wet" sugar for a "dry" one, you should reduce your liquids by an equal measure. Observe the dough as it mixes. If it needs that missing moisture, you can always add it back in during the kneading cycle.

Handy hint of the day: When measuring sticky sugars such as honey, molasses, barley malt syrup, etc., coat your measuring spoon with a small amount of oil first. This will make the sweetener slide easily out of the spoon.

The following is a list of the sugars we were able to locate in grocery and health food stores (we have separated the "dry" granular sugars from the "wet" syrups):

GRANULATED WHITE SUGAR

• Table sugar is almost pure sucrose and has little nutritional value.

• Adding sugar to bread will help preserve its freshness, give color to the crust, and make each slice moist and tender.

• Do not substitute powdered sugar for granulated white sugar in bread recipes. Powdered sugar contains cornstarch.

BROWN SUGAR

• Brown sugar is essentially granulated white sugar crystals with a thin coating of molasses.

• The difference between light and dark brown sugars is the amount of molasses added.

• 1 tablespoon white sugar = 1 packed tablespoon brown sugar.

• Brown sugar will slightly increase the acidic environment in your doughs.

FRUCTOSE

• Fructose, in its natural state, is the sugar found in fruits, vegetables, and honey. Commercial fructose, however, is usually obtained by breaking down sucrose into its basic elements—glucose and fructose—then separating out the fructose. Fructose created this way is a highly refined sugar, even more so than granulated white sugar.

• Fructose is almost 75 percent sweeter than granulated white sugar, giving you more sweetening power for fewer calories. To replace the sugar in recipes with fructose: 1 tablespoon sugar = a heaping 1½ teaspoons fructose.

TURBINADO SUGAR

• Turbinado sugar is a partially refined sugar similar to brown sugar.

• 1 tablespoon granulated white sugar = 1 tablespoon turbinado sugar.

DATE SUGAR

• Surprisingly, since dates have the highest sugar content of any fruit, this sugar made from ground, dried dates is only moderately sweet.

MAPLE SUGAR

• Maple sugar is made from maple syrup that has been boiled down to a sugary state, then dehydrated. It is very, very sweet.

SUCANAT

• Sucanat stands for "sugar cane natural." It's the closest thing to "natural" sugar. It is sugar cane juice in a granulated form. Unlike nutritionally deficient table sugar, Sucanat retains all the sugar cane's vitamins and minerals.

• Sucanat has the same sweetening power as granulated sugar. 1 tablespoon sugar = 1 tablespoon Sucanat

HONEY

• Honeys vary widely in their sweetness. They range from 1½ times sweeter than table sugar all the way down to less sweet than table sugar.

• When replacing sugar with honey, start with a guideline of 1 tablespoon sugar = 2 teaspoons honey, then adjust to suit your taste if the honey you're using isn't particularly sweet.

• Honey does an even better job of preserving a bread's moisture than

table sugar. In fact, because of its moisture-attracting properties, on humid days any breads containing honey will actually absorb moisture from the air.

• The darker the honey, the stronger and more acidic the taste.

• Honey will contribute some acid to your bread doughs.

• With age and cool temperatures, honey will eventually crystallize. To return it to its liquid state temporarily, you can either place it in a pan of hot water or warm it briefly in the microwave.

• Along the same lines, on cold winter days when the honey is so thick it will hardly budge, or when you're down to the bottom of the jar and want to capture every last drop, place your container of honey in the microwave (or in a pan of hot water) to warm it up and make it easier to pour. The average jar of honey will warm up in just 20 or 30 seconds on HIGH in the microwave. (For the "dregs," about 5 seconds should do it.)

• Store honey in a cool, dry, dark place. Keep tightly covered.

• If raw, unpasteurized honey is left exposed to the air, on humid days it will absorb water. If it absorbs a great deal of water, yeasts will grow and spoil it, turning its sugar into alcohol and carbon dioxide.

• If using raw, unpasteurized honey, it's best to heat it first (no higher than 180°F) to destroy the enzymes in it that may play havoc with your bread dough.

• We think proper homage should be paid to the incredible honey bee. Each bee works **an entire lifetime** just to produce one teaspoon of honey! So, please include the tiny honey bee next time you offer up high praise for that marvelous loaf of honey wheat bread you just enjoyed. What a gift!

MOLASSES

• During processing, sugar is spun in large centrifuges. The liquid that is spun out is boiled several times and yields different grades of molasses.

• Molasses is not as sweet as granulated sugar; 1 tablespoon sugar = 4 teaspoons molasses.

• Molasses will increase the acid level in your bread dough. To neutralize it, you can add a pinch of baking soda, if desired. (Since yeast prefers an acidic environment, we suggest you first try the recipe without the added baking soda.)

• We recommend the milder-flavored unsulphured variety of molasses.

• The shelf life of an opened jar of molasses is one year.

MAPLE SYRUP

• The sap from maple trees is boiled down to a syrup state.

• Maple syrup is sweeter than granulated sugar but not as sweet as most honeys. 1 tablespoon sugar = ¾ tablespoon maple syrup.

• The lighter the color, the better the grade of maple syrup.

• Once opened, maple syrup should be stored in the refrigerator to inhibit the growth of any mold on top.

• If a mold develops, don't panic. Simply pour it off, strain the syrup through a sieve lined with cheesecloth, then bring it to a boil on the stove or in the microwave before pouring it back into the bottle.

SORGHUM

• This syrup is similar to molasses but thinner and not as sweet.

• Sorghum is not a by-product of sugar refining; rather, it is derived from crushing the stalks of the sorghum plant, then boiling down its juices.

CORN SYRUP

• This is a sweet syrup that is made from the starch in corn. When used in breads, it helps keep them fresh and moist.

• Corn syrup has only half the sweetness of sugar: 1 tablespoon sugar = 2 tablespoons corn syrup.

BARLEY MALT SYRUP

• Barley malt syrup is a complex sugar made from sprouted barley. It tastes like a cross between honey and molasses.

• Its sugar profile is: 77% maltose, 15% glucose, 7% sucrose, and 1% fructose.

• The jar we use states that you can substitute barley malt syrup one to one for honey or molasses. In our bread baking, however, we found better results using half that amount. In other words: 1 tablespoon honey = ½ tablespoon (1½ teaspoons) barley malt syrup.

• "Hop-flavored" barley malt syrup is sold for brewing and is quite bitter tasting, not something you'd want to add to your breads as a sweetener.

• Barley malt syrup has been heated in processing so it contains none of the active malt enzymes found in diastatic malt powder (see "Dough Enhancers" on page 81) that would alter the chemistry of your bread baking.

• Once opened, store barley malt syrup in the refrigerator.

BROWN RICE SYRUP

• This thick, mild-tasting syrup is a product of fermented brown rice. You can use it as you would barley malt syrup.

• Rice syrup has a high proportion of complex carbohydrates; it does not enter the blood stream as rapidly as simple sugars.

LIQUID FRUIT CONCENTRATES

• Products such as Fruit Sweet (pear, peach, and pineapple juice concentrates) and Fruit Source (grape juice concentrate and rice syrup) can be used to sweeten your breads. They contain no refined sugars.

STORAGE

• All sugars should be stored in airtight containers. They are hygroscopic (moisture-attracting) and will absorb water from the air.

Eggs

• Eggs add liquid, color, structure, nutrients, flavor, and tenderness to breads.

• Each large egg is equivalent to a scant ¼ cup liquid.

• Brown or white eggs can be used.

• If you have a bread that's a reluctant riser, replace ¼ cup of the liquid with a large egg.

• Breads containing eggs have a tendency to dry out faster than other breads. Adding extra fat to the recipe compensates for this tendency.

• To bring an egg to room temperature quickly, submerge it in hot tap water for a few moments.

• You can test an egg's freshness by submerging it in a pan of water. If it floats, it's not fresh.

Gluten
—◆◆◆—

There's a great deal of confusion over the terms "gluten," "vital wheat gluten," "vital wheat gluten flour," and "gluten flour." The terms are often used interchangeably. Our phone calls to numerous mills and distributors revealed that even the experts had slightly different definitions. We found the same to be true in published works. So, while we continue to pursue *the* final authority on the subject, we offer you these interim guidelines:

GLUTEN

• Gluten is the protein found mainly in wheat flour, and it is a key element in yeast breads. It provides the bread's framework.

• Flours with a high gluten content make the best bread flours. Conversely, those flours low in gluten, such as rye, barley, buckwheat, millet, etc., need a "boost" of added gluten to rise adequately. Changing the wheat/non-wheat flour ratio will help.

• Breads made without a bread machine require a 50 percent minimum of wheat flour. In the bread machine, we found the ratios 2:1, 2½:1, and 3:1 to be workable (i.e., 2, 2½, or 3 cups of wheat flour for every cup of non-wheat flour).

VITAL WHEAT GLUTEN

• The gluten in wheat flour can actually be isolated and removed in a long process that involves washing the starch out of the flour. What remains is pure 100 percent gluten. It is then dried, ground, packaged, and sold as "vital wheat gluten."

• Vital wheat gluten is not a flour; it's an additive that gives the bread more strength, structure, and a finer texture, and usually increases its height. Vital wheat gluten is especially useful when baking with whole grains that are low in gluten and would otherwise bake up as "mini boulders" in the bread machine.

• Vital wheat gluten is often referred to simply as "gluten."

• The distributors of this pure gluten recommend using 1 teaspoon vital wheat gluten per cup of flour in white breads and 1½ teaspoons per cup of flour in whole-grain breads. For example, in a recipe that calls for 2 cups whole wheat flour and 1 cup bread flour, add 4½ teaspoons vital wheat gluten.

• Gluten absorbs water and adding a large quantity of vital wheat gluten can dry out your dough. Observe it as it mixes; if the dough is dry or stiff, add 1 to 2 tablespoons more water.

• Vital wheat gluten's shelf life, stored at room temperature, unopened, is two years. Opened, it will last about a year when kept in the refrigerator or freezer.

VITAL WHEAT GLUTEN FLOUR

• Sometimes, not all the starch is removed in the washing process. The result is a vital wheat gluten that is about 75 percent gluten and 25 percent flour.

• This, too, is an additive though some people do bake it up as a meat substitute.

• People refer to it as both "gluten" and "gluten flour."

• This is the gluten we usually purchase. We refer to this vital wheat gluten flour as "gluten" in our recipes and throughout this book whenever we suggest adding gluten to flour. If you purchase the pure vital wheat gluten instead of the vital wheat gluten flour, follow the guidelines on the package rather than our suggested amounts. (You will use less.)

• We've learned that adding 1½ teaspoons vital wheat gluten flour per cup of flour in white breads and 1 tablespoon vital wheat gluten flour per cup of flour in whole-grain breads works best. For example, if the recipe listed 1 cup of bread flour, 1 cup of whole wheat flour, and 1 cup of rye flour, we added 3 tablespoons vital wheat gluten flour as well.

• As with vital wheat gluten, when adding vital wheat gluten flour to your dough, you may also need to increase the liquid by 1 or 2 tablespoons while it is kneading.

GLUTEN FLOUR

• The biggest confusion lies in the definition of gluten flour. We've heard and read it's a flour with a gluten content of 14 percent (bread flour), a flour comprised of 80 percent gluten and 20 percent flour, and everything in between! The most common definition seemed to be a 50 percent gluten, 50 percent all-purpose flour.

• We feel that the only way to make sense of it all is to know the gluten content when you purchase "gluten flour." The lower the gluten content, the more you'll need to add to boost your bread.

Dough Enhancers
<hr>

Dough "enhancers" are optional supplements that can increase gluten strength, aid the yeast's fermentation, produce a more yeast-friendly environment, convert starch into sugar, or help emulsify oils. Their use will often result in taller, lighter loaves and/or breads that will stay fresher longer.

Most dough enhancers contain all-natural ingredients but there are a few that contain artificial ingredients. It's fun to experiment with them, but if your main purpose in owning a bread machine is to escape the chemically laden commercial breads, adding some of these extras to your homemade breads just doesn't make sense. Frankly, fresh home-baked bread seldom needs anything more than extra gluten once in a while. Don't mess with a good thing!

GLUTEN

• Companies such as Arrowhead Mills and Bob's Red Mill package and sell vital wheat gluten and vital wheat gluten flour. Some health food stores also sell it in their bulk bins.

• To create taller, lighter breads you can add gluten to your dough. It's most often used in whole-grain breads, which tend to bake up small and dense in the bread machine.

• See page 79 for recommended amounts.

DIASTATIC MALT POWDER (MALTED BARLEY FLOUR)

• Malted barley or wheat powder is created from sprouted wheat or barley kernels that have been roasted, ground, filtered, and then dehydrated.

• Diastatic malt powder (dimalt) contains enzymes that break down the flour's starch and convert it into sugar (food for the yeast).

• It improves the bread's flavor, gives it a better texture, and helps it stay fresh longer.

• It should be added only in tiny quantities: Start by adding ¼ teaspoon per loaf. You can increase it by ¼ teaspoon each time you try a certain recipe until you notice your dough developing gummy spots, then cut back the quantity. A few experimental tries and you will find the right amount for your breads.

• If you add too little, the bread will be a sickly pale color. Add too much and the dough will turn very sticky and not bake up properly.

• Since diastatic malt continues to convert starch into sugar during rising, do not use it in any long-rising breads such as French or sourdough.

• Adding this all-natural product makes it possible to reduce or eliminate the use of sugar in bread recipes.

• If you're interested in a challenge, you can create your own diastatic barley or wheat malt. *The Laurel's Kitchen Bread Book*, by Laurel Robertson (New York: Random House, 1984), gives full directions for sprouting, drying, and producing your own diastatic malt on pages 274 and 275. (You do need some type of grain grinder to mill the dried sprouts.)

• If your health food store doesn't carry diastatic malt powder, try one of the companies listed in our Sources section (page 189).

• It keeps well in the freezer.

LECITHIN

• Lecithin, an emulsifier that will delay the staling process in breads, is available in granular or liquid form.

• Lecithin is found naturally in egg yolks and soy beans.

• One tablespoon of lecithin granules contains 50 calories.

• We've done numerous tests using lecithin and it's been our experience that when combined with additional gluten, lecithin seems to enhance gluten's power to give added height to breads. Those breads with both gluten and lecithin added were measurably taller than those made with just gluten. Breads baked with added lecithin but no extra gluten were no different from breads baked without either lecithin or gluten. Our bottom line: Lecithin and gluten combined produced the highest loaves. Lecithin by itself, while it may have added to the keeping quality of the bread, did not increase the height of the bread.

• Use ¼ teaspoon lecithin (granular or liquid) per cup of flour.

• If you use liquid lecithin, which is very sticky, it helps to oil the measuring spoon first.

ASCORBIC ACID (VITAMIN C)

• Ascorbic acid strengthens the protein in flour and gives the loaf more volume.

• Some bread flours contain either potassium bromate or ascorbic acid to give added strength to the dough.

• Testing that we have done using 150 mg ascorbic acid per cup of flour has resulted in much higher loaves of bread.

• You can purchase pure vitamin C (ascorbic acid) in crystal, tablet, or capsule form at any well-stocked pharmacy or health food store.

• It will require a little bit of math on your part to calculate how much of the crystals, crushed tablet, or capsule contents you will need to equal 150 mg. For instance, we purchased a jar of vitamin C crystals that contained 5,000 mg pure vitamin C per teaspoon. To reduce it down to a 150 mg amount, we had to use 1/32 of a teaspoon! It hardly seems possible that such a minute amount can make any difference in the size of the bread, but it does.

POTASSIUM BROMATE

• Bread flour with this additive is known as "bromated" flour.

• Potassium bromate is added to some bread flours to give the gluten added strength, which in turn will result in taller, lighter loaves of bread.

• Some studies indicate that potassium bromate is carcinogenic. In California, any flour containing potassium bromate must have a health warning included.

• Ascorbic acid can be used in place of potassium bromate.

COMMERCIAL DOUGH ENHANCERS

• There is a commercial dough enhancer on the market that contains a little bit of everything: whey, soy lecithin, tofu, citric acid, yeast, sea salt, natural spice blend, cornstarch, ascorbic acid. On the container, the recommended amount is 1 teaspoon per cup of flour. We have not tried this product (its name is "Dough Enhancer"), yet know others who are pleased with the results.

• If you can't find Dough Enhancer in your stores, Magic Mill sells it directly (see Sources, page 189).

• There are also products, such as S500, that commercial bakeries use to enhance breads. Some may eventually find their way to the retail market as more and more of us bake our own breads.

Sourdough

A sourdough starter is the "sour" in sourdough. It's basically a combination of flour, liquid, and yeast stored in a loosely covered jar or crock in the refrigerator. Frequent use or regular feeding keeps it alive. Some starters have been known to survive for generations!

There are probably as many sourdough starter recipes as there are wrinkles on an elephant. We won't go into them here, but we encourage you to find a good sourdough cookbook and try a few of the different types. For now, we'd simply like to offer a few tips and facts we've learned from our baking.

USING A STARTER

• Bring refrigerated starter to room temperature before using it. You can place it in a bowl of warm water if you're in a hurry or you can leave it out overnight if you plan to use it in the morning.

• Like most things in life, sourdough starter gets better with age. So don't be discouraged if your first breads don't quite live up to your sourest expectations. Just keep baking with it and very soon you'll notice it taking on its own tangy personality.

• Experiment. Use your sourdough starter in some of your favorite recipes. Rye breads are especially yummy when soured. If your starter is roughly half liquid and half flour, when you add starter to a recipe, consider half the amount of starter used as liquid and reduce the liquid in the recipe by that amount. In other words, if you choose to add 1 cup of sourdough starter to a rye bread recipe that lists 1¼ cups water, count the 1 cup starter as ½ cup liquid and deduct that amount from your 1¼ cups water. (For that recipe your liquids would be 1 cup sourdough starter and ¾ cup water.)

MAINTAINING A STARTER

• After each use, the starter needs to be replenished with equal amounts of liquid and flour. Do so, then cover it loosely and leave it out at room temperature for several hours until it increases and turns spongy-looking. Stir it down, then refrigerate.

• Your starter should always be kept in the refrigerator or freezer. The exceptions: those first few days as it's developing, the few hours before it's used, and the few hours after it's replenished or fed.

• Feed your starter once a month if you are not using it. Add equal amounts of flour and warm liquid (90° to 100°F). Cover loosely and allow it to stand in a warm location (70° to 95°F) until it expands and turns spongy-looking. Stir it down and then place it in the refrigerator, loosely covered.

• Remove the starter from its container every so often and give the container a good wash job in hot water.

• Sourdough starter ages best when handled with tender, loving care (don't we all!). So, do remember to feed it. If you're going to be gone or know you won't be baking with your starter for an extended period of time, you can freeze it. When you choose to use it again, allow your starter to sit at room temperature for 24 hours to thaw out and come back to life.

• If, after freezing or several weeks of non-use, your starter looks a little sluggish and isn't displaying its usual bubbly personality, reserve 1 or 2 tablespoons of the starter in a separate bowl and pour the rest away. Thoroughly wash the container and place the reserved starter back into the clean container. Add 1 cup warm liquid (90° to 100°F) and 1 cup flour. Cover loosely and let it stand in a warm place (70° to 95°F) for several hours until bubbly and a clear liquid begins to form on top. You may need to repeat this process once or twice to bring it back to its bubbly, sour-smelling self again.

• To maintain a 70° to 95°F temperature for your starter, place it in any warm location such as an oven with the pilot light on, a warm kitchen, on top of the water heater or refrigerator, in the sunshine during the day, in a bowl filled with water set on a warming tray, or directly on a heating pad. We've even heard of people placing starter or rising dough in a warm car. That sounds like a great idea until the one time you forget all about it and it bubbles out all over the upholstery! Try explaining that sour odor every time it's your turn to drive in the car pool.

HOW TO MAKE THE SOUREST SOURDOUGH

• Remove your starter from the refrigerator and bring it up to room temperature.

• Combine the amount of starter called for in your recipe with the liquid and two-thirds of the flour.

• Stir, cover the bowl, and allow it to sit at room temperature for at least 24 hours.

• Combine this mixture in your bread machine pan with the remaining ingredients in the recipe.

• Potato starters are usually sweeter starters. Those made with skim milk and yogurt are the sourest.

MISCELLANEOUS FACTS AND HELPFUL HINTS

• Use only wooden utensils and glass or ceramic containers. The starter will corrode metal.

• The grayish or yellowish liquid that rises to the top is the "hooch." Just stir it back in before using your starter.

• Do not keep your starter in a container that is tightly sealed. The accumulating gasses could shatter the jar.

• If you just don't seem to have the knack for getting a starter started, don't despair. Nobody's going to show up on your doorstep pointing fingers and snickering at you. The world doesn't even have to know. Instead, just tiptoe down to your favorite gourmet cooking store and pick up a packet of instant sourdough starter. Mix it up as directed and you'll be in sourdough heaven in no time!

• You can use your sourdough starter to create sublime pancakes and waffles, too.

WHEN TO DISCARD YOUR STARTER

• If your starter turns pink or orange or develops mold, discard it and start again.

• If you neglected your starter for months on end, tried to resuscitate it but to no avail, it's time to bid it adieu and start over.

We hate to be the bearer of bad news, but if you had your heart set on duplicating the incredible sourdoughs of San Francisco fame, you can forget it. To begin with, you'd have to have a starter that was an offspring of theirs. When was the last time you saw any of the famous bakeries handing out starter samples? Then you'd actually have to live in the Bay Area to capture the same airborne yeasts, use the same water, and duplicate the remaining ingredients. But pick your chin up off the ground. You can still create a little slice of heaven with your very own sourdough ingredients!

Miscellaneous Ingredients

CARAMEL COLORING

• This is added to pumpernickels, black breads, and some European peasant breads to give them their characteristic dark color.

• It's simple to make and even simpler to buy (in its concentrated form from a bakery).

• **Caution: Read the entire directions before you begin!**

In a small, very heavy saucepan, combine ½ cup sugar and 2 tablespoons water. Bring mixture to a boil over medium heat; let boil for about 15 minutes, stirring frequently with a wooden spoon. (Don't be alarmed. It will harden, remelt, and smoke during this process.) Remove pan from heat when the mixture turns a very dark molasses color. **VERY IMPORTANT: ALLOW THE MIXTURE TO COOL COMPLETELY (10 MINUTES) BEFORE ADDING MORE WATER. YOU WILL AVOID AN EXPLOSIVE SITUATION THAT COULD LEAVE YOU BADLY BURNED.** (At this point, you may think you've ruined your pan because the sugar is now a very thick glob in the bottom of it. Have faith. Keep going.) When the mixture is cool, add ¼ cup boiling water. Return the pan to the stove, stir over medium heat for about five minutes until it becomes a smooth, thin liquid. Cool completely; store in a covered jar at room temperature indefinitely. Add 1 tablespoon caramel coloring to your bread doughs to give them a dark color (it won't add sweetness). You can also brush it on pumpernickel and black breads as a glaze before baking them in the oven.

CHILI PEPPERS

• If you like your chiles on the mild side, select fresh Anaheim chiles. They are the long, tapered, green chiles in the produce section. You can also buy mild green chiles in a can.

• For lovers of the hot and spicy variety, choose either fresh or canned jalapeños. They are small, dark green chiles.

• Hotter still are serrano chiles. They are dark green, smaller and thinner than the jalapeño peppers.

• The chili pepper's "heat" is in the seeds and ribs. Since canned diced jalapeños include the seeds and ribs, we found they produced a hotter bread than the fresh jalapeño peppers with seeds and ribs removed.

• When working with chili peppers, avoid touching your face, eyes, or mouth. Wash your hands well when done. If you have sensitive skin, wear rubber gloves.

• A general rule of thumb: "The smaller the chili, the hotter the fire." Keep that in mind the next time you're in a Mexican restaurant and a friend dares you to munch on that *tiny* little chili pepper.

DAIRY PRODUCTS

• We've discovered that several products vary greatly in density, texture, acidity levels, etc., from brand to brand and from one part of the country to another. These items include sour cream, cottage cheese, buttermilk, ricotta cheese, yogurt, and applesauce. After a trip to the east coast, Lois learned that the sour cream her sons and their families were using in their breads was twice as thick as the brand she used. It made a big difference in the final results. Buttermilk varies widely, too, as we learned from the network of bread bakers on a computer bulletin board who tested our DeDe's Buttermilk Bread. They ended up with tall loaves, tiny loaves and everything in between. The different brands of buttermilk (liquid and powder) with their varying levels of acidity seemed to be the culprit. So, if you're having trouble duplicating a particular bread, there's a possibility it's a variation in the composition of the ingredients that's at fault.

FRUIT

• When a recipe calls for ripe bananas, make sure they are very ripe. They should have dark spots on the peel. If they are not ripe, they won't mash up properly and provide the necessary "liquid."

• Adding fruit, with its natural pectin, will improve the keeping quality of your breads.

• To help keep fragile fruits such as berries intact, freeze them first. Spread them out on a baking sheet and freeze them individually. Once frozen, place them in a plastic bag or container until needed. Add them to the bread dough in their frozen state.

• If you have a dehydrator or convection oven, try drying your fruits first. They will hold up better in the dough and give a more intense flavor.

• If you add dried fruits, you may also need to increase the liquid slightly.

• Before squeezing the juice from a fresh orange or lemon, remove the zest first either by grating or with a vegetable peeler and then chopping it up in a small food processor. Freeze the peel to have on hand when you want to add a little zip to a particular bread.

• When removing the zest of any citrus fruit, remove only the colored outer skin. The white pith underneath is bitter and not desirable.

• Heat lemons and oranges briefly in the microwave before squeezing. They'll produce more juice.

NUTS

• Almonds, brazil nuts, filberts, peanuts, pecans, pine nuts, and walnuts are wonderful additions to homemade breads, especially fruit breads.

• Pecans and filberts add their own extra sweetness while walnuts have a more bitter flavor, which balances well with the sweetest fruit breads.

• Nuts contain natural oils that will turn rancid when stored at warm temperatures for any length of time. To preserve their freshness, store them in the refrigerator or freezer. A few rancid nuts can ruin your perfect loaf.

• Toasting nuts and seeds on a cookie sheet in a 350°F oven for 8 to 10 minutes will bring out their flavors. Watch them carefully to avoid scorching.

PACKAGED BREAD MACHINE MIXES

• We've tried a few of the packaged mixes now on the market and though they aren't quite as wonderful tasting as what you can make with your own fresh ingredients, they are certainly acceptable and can have a place in the bread machine baker's pantry. Their best features: most bake up beautifully (we tried them in several different machines), they're incredibly convenient (all you do is add water and the packet of yeast), and they are ideal for the Delayed Bake Cycle. For those reasons, we think they'd be perfect as part of a starter kit for the brand new bread machine owner. Producing nice-looking loaves of bread the first few times would instill some confidence in the hesitant bread baker, plus encourage the new owner to use different cycles on his or her machine. For the experienced bread baker, the mixes are handy to have around for those moments when 30 seconds before dashing out the door in the morning is about all the time you can allocate for baking your daily loaf of bread.

POTATOES

• Potatoes, either instant or freshly mashed, are a boon to homemade breads. They add moisture, a naturally sweet, rich flavor, and seem to give the yeast a boost, as well.

• We have added up to ½ cup of plain mashed potatoes in some recipes.

Prepared mashed potatoes contain a great deal of moisture so when you add them to your recipes, reduce your liquids by at least ¼ cup to start. If the dough appears dry, add more liquid 1 tablespoon at a time while it's kneading.

RAISINS

• For added flavor, soak raisins in vanilla, rum, brandy, or dust with cinnamon before adding them to a recipe.

• You can store them in the refrigerator. Cold raisins will hold up better during the kneading process.

SEEDS

• Caraway, poppy, sesame, and sunflower seeds are the most popular seeds used in bread baking. Though millet is actually a grain, it can be added to breads as a seed.

• We prefer the raw, unsalted sunflower seeds from the bins at our local health food store. They have a mild, sweet flavor. If you can locate only the toasted, salted variety, reduce the amount of salt in your recipe.

• Seeds, like nuts, contain natural oils that will turn rancid quickly if exposed to warm temperatures. It is best to store them in the refrigerator or freezer to prevent rancidity.

• Toasting millet, sesame, and sunflower seeds in a Teflon-coated skillet over medium heat for a few minutes will accentuate their flavor. Watch closely to ensure they don't burn and turn bitter.

Substitutions
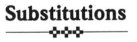

BREAD FLOUR

• To create your own bread flour, add 1½ teaspoons gluten to each cup of all-purpose flour.

BUTTERMILK

• To create a mock buttermilk, add 1 tablespoon lemon juice or distilled white vinegar to 1 cup warm nonfat or lowfat milk. Stir and let the mixture clabber for about five minutes.

• Replace the buttermilk with water and add 1 tablespoon powdered buttermilk to the dry ingredients for every ¼ cup buttermilk you are replacing. For example, if the recipe calls for ¾ cup buttermilk, replace it with ¾ cup water and add 3 tablespoons buttermilk powder to the dry ingredients. (Note: When substituting powdered buttermilk in a recipe, omit the baking soda if it is a listed ingredient. The powder is less acidic than fresh buttermilk and the baking soda further neutralizes it—not a desirable goal when working with yeast.)

• Substitute plain yogurt in equal measure for buttermilk.

EGGS

• There are many low- and non-cholesterol egg substitutes in the milk and freezer sections of grocery stores today. (They do contain eggs.) Add a scant ¼ cup of those products to replace one large egg in a recipe.

• Two egg whites equal one whole egg.

• For each large egg, substitute 3 tablespoons water and 2 teaspoons Ener-G Egg Replacer (powdered non-egg product).

• You can omit eggs in recipes by replacing each with a scant ¼ cup of water.

FATS

• Replace fats in bread recipes with an equal amount of unsweetened applesauce, or any other puréed fruit, and reduce the recipe's liquid by an equal amount.

• In some recipes you can omit the fat without replacement.

• Butter, margarine, oil, and solid shortening can be used interchangeably in most recipes. If you substitute a liquid for a solid, observe the dough as it's mixing. If it looks too wet, add 1 to 2 tablespoons more flour as needed.

• Products such as Wonderslim replace fat with all-natural products such as water and dried plums. For every tablespoon of fat in the recipe, use ½ tablespoon (1½ teaspoons) Wonderslim. You can find Wonderslim in major grocery stores, usually near the sugar substitutes.

FRUITS AND VEGETABLES

• If you decide to add fresh fruit or vegetables to a recipe, as a general rule of thumb consider them to be half liquid and deduct that amount of liquid from your recipe. Adding 1 cup of chopped apples means reducing the liquid in the recipe by ½ cup. Observe the dough as it mixes and adjust the balance by adding either more liquid or more flour, 1 tablespoon at a time, as needed.

HERBS

• When substituting fresh for dried herbs, triple the amount. 1 tablespoon dried herbs equals 3 tablespoons fresh.

MILK

• You may use any milk interchangeably: whole, lowfat, 1%, or skim.

• Replace the milk with water and add ¾ to 1 tablespoon nonfat dry milk to the dry ingredients for every ¼ cup milk you are replacing.

• Non-dairy milk products such as soy milk, rice milk, etc., may be used in equal measure to replace milk in recipes.

• Powdered soy milk or tofu milk powder may be used instead of nonfat dry milk; follow the package directions.

• Equal measures of vegetable cooking water, fruit juices, vegetable juices, flat beer, and just plain water are all viable substitutions for milk in most recipes. Use your best judgment when combining various flavors, but don't hesitate to experiment!

ONION

• You can substitute 1 tablespoon dried onion flakes for ¼ cup chopped fresh onion. You will also need to add 1 to 2 tablespoons water for every ¼ cup chopped fresh onion omitted. Observe the dough while it is mixing and add the water as needed.

SALT

• So far, there is no salt substitute that has the right properties for use in baking breads.

• A "lite" salt must contain both potassium chloride and sodium; plain potassium chloride will not work. Morton Lite Salt is the only brand we've been able to locate so far that fits the bill. Use it measure for measure in your bread recipes.

• You can use either table salt or sea salt in bread recipes.

• If you prefer to use coarse kosher salt, increase the amount by 1 teaspoon to allow for its coarser texture.

• DO NOT use rock salt as a substitute for coarse kosher salt. It is meant for ice cream makers and paved highways, not our tummies.

SOUR CREAM

• Replace all or part of whole sour cream with plain yogurt, reduced-fat sour cream, or fat-free sour cream.

• To make a mock lowfat sour cream: In a blender or food processor, combine 1 cup lowfat cottage cheese, ¼ cup buttermilk or plain yogurt, and 1 tablespoon lemon juice. Blend for a few seconds.

SOURDOUGH

• If you want to add sourdough starter to a recipe, count half of it as liquid and deduct that amount from the liquid listed in the recipe. If you use 1 cup of starter, reduce the liquid in the recipe by ½ cup.

SUGAR

• For a different flavor, you can substitute an equal measure of brown sugar for white. (Brown sugar should always be packed firmly into the measuring spoon or cup when it is measured.)

• Do not substitute powdered sugar for table sugar.

• One tablespoon of granulated white sugar equals the following:
  1 packed tablespoon of brown sugar
  A heaping 1½ teaspoons fructose
  1 tablespoon turbinado sugar
  1 tablespoon Sucanat
  2 teaspoons honey
  4 teaspoons molasses
  2 tablespoons corn syrup
  ¾ tablespoon maple syrup

• Other substitutes for table sugar include: sorghum, maple sugar, date sugar, barley malt syrup, brown rice syrup, pureed fruits, frozen fruit concentrates, Fruit Sweet, jams and jellies.

• As of this writing, Sweet One and Sugar Twin are the only sugar substitutes in the grocery stores that can be used in baking. Each packet is equivalent to 2 teaspoons sugar; however, we found that using the full amount of Sugar Twin produced too sweet a loaf for our tastes. If you, like us, prefer your bread less sweet, use half the recommended amount of Sugar Twin.

• You can omit the sugar in most recipes and replace it with diastatic malt powder. You use much less malt powder than sugar. Our best test results were achieved by using ¼ teaspoon malt powder in the 1-pound (2 cups flour) loaves and ½ teaspoon in the 1½-pound (3 cups flour) loaves.

WHOLE WHEAT FLOUR

• If you have no whole wheat flour on hand, you can create your own. In the bottom of a measuring cup (for dry ingredients), place 1 teaspoon wheat germ and 2½ tablespoons wheat bran. Fill the cup with unbleached wheat flour and level.

WHOLE WHEAT BREAD FLOUR

• To create "homemade" whole wheat bread flour, follow the preceding directions for whole wheat flour but replace the unbleached flour with bread flour.

YEAST

• One ¼-ounce packet of yeast equals 2¼ teaspoons of yeast.

• One ⅗-ounce cake of compressed yeast is equal to one ¼-ounce packet of active dry yeast.

❖❖❖ 4 ❖❖❖

How to Adjust Recipes
to Fit Your
Dietary Needs

The Nutritional
Benefits of Homemade Bread
❖❖❖

We're always amazed when people make the remark, "Oh, I can't buy a bread machine. I'd end up eating too much bread!" Has anybody checked out the new USDA Food Guide Pyramid lately? The Basic Four Food Groups are a thing of the past. The foundation of this healthier eating guideline is the bread, cereal, rice, and pasta group—six to eleven servings daily! Haven't we

■ 95 ■

all known it for years . . . we consume too many high-fat meat and dairy products and not nearly enough grains, fruits, and vegetables? Breathes there a soul who isn't aware it's time to trim the fat? That means it's time to rethink some lifelong bad habits. Instead of being the main portion of our meals, meat and dairy products should be used as supplements to meals centered around grains, beans, fruits, and vegetables. And any healthy vegetarian will chime in that it's possible to do without meat entirely (and dairy if you're a vegan)!

Much like the baked potato, bread is often maligned as being fattening. It's not the bread that's fattening, it's what you put on it! An entire 1½-pound loaf of whole wheat bread might contain only 1¼ tablespoons of fat, 1½ tablespoons of sugar, 3 cups of flour, and an egg or a cup of lowfat milk . . . not too bad when you divide that by 12 or 14 slices. In fact, for those of us who have been up and down the scale like a yo-yo, wholesome bread can be a newfound "friend." If you ask the waiter to remove the bread basket in a restaurant; if you remove the top half of the bun before eating a hamburger; if you eat your sandwiches open-faced in an effort to cut calories, it may be time to rethink your tactics. Filling up on the wonderful breads and rolls many restaurants now serve (sans butter, of course) can certainly take the edge off your appetite. By the time your higher-calorie, higher-fat entrée appears, you're much less likely to overindulge. In fact, it's quite possible to dine out and be very satisfied with good bread, a dinner salad, and a light appetizer rather than a full-course meal. As for eating burgers or sandwiches open-faced, a wiser move is to reduce the size of the hamburger patty and to make your sandwiches with thick slices of whole-grain bread and very little meat filling. You'll get all the flavor, more satiety, less fat, and fewer calories.

If you have other special dietary requirements, it's possible to adjust the bread recipes to better suit your nutritional needs. In this section we will give you plenty of tips on how to reduce or eliminate fat, sugar, salt, cholesterol, and animal and dairy products in your daily bread. There are also computer software programs that will provide a nutritional analysis of your recipes. This may be a useful aid for those of you who closely monitor your meals.

Do you recall how we described gluten as being an essential ingredient in the bread-baking process? In this chapter we have to modify that statement. People with wheat and gluten intolerances are baking gluten-free breads all the time in their bread machines! That came as quite a shock to us. Only a few months ago we would have dismissed it as impossible. We hope this news will reach others with the same condition and open new doors for them. Until now they've been faced with paying premium prices for their gluten-free breads.

So, the good news is, people with heart conditions, weight problems, diabetes, high cholesterol, celiac sprue, wheat allergies, lactose intolerance, and those who choose not to eat dairy or animal products can still enjoy great, wholesome, preservative-free breads from their bread machines without tremendous cost or major effort. Bread is good for you! To the person who's afraid to buy a bread machine and exclaims, "I'd end up eating too much bread," we say, "GREAT!"

Ways to Reduce or Eliminate Fats in Bread
❖❖❖

• You can replace the fat in most loaves with an equal measure of unsweetened applesauce. Diana Lewis, a friend of ours, has this suggestion: Freeze your applesauce in 1-tablespoon quantities in ice-cube trays. Once frozen, pop them into a heavy plastic bag and store them in the freezer until needed.

• Instead of applesauce, you can use any other unsweetened fruit you have on hand. Simply purée it in a blender or food processor. Note: When testing applesauce and puréed fruit as replacements for solid fats such as butter, margarine, or shortening, we noticed that our breads had better texture when we reduced the liquid in the recipes by the same amount. In other words, when we replaced 2 tablespoons of butter with 2 tablespoons of applesauce, our breads were coarse textured and chewy. When we made that same substitution but also reduced the liquid in the recipe by 2 tablespoons, our bread was much finer textured and very similar to the original recipe.

• We've also discovered that you can simply omit the fat in many recipes without any replacement. Of course, those breads are not as tender and turn stale quickly.

• Lite margarine may be used in place of regular margarine. It contains more water than regular margarine so you may need to reduce the liquids by a few teaspoons if you find your breads have a coarser texture when using lite margarine.

• Fat-substitute products such as Wonderslim contain all-natural ingredients such as water and dried plums. The directions say to replace the fat in the recipe with one half the amount of Wonderslim.

• Another ingredient in your bread that contains fat is milk. By substituting nonfat milk, fruit juices, or vegetable juices for whole milk you've eliminated another source of fat.

• If a recipe calls for sour cream, consider plain yogurt as a substitute. There are also reduced-fat and fat-free sour creams that perform equally well.

• Egg substitutes found in the milk or freezer section of the grocery store are lower in fat than whole fresh eggs. Replacing one whole egg with two egg whites is another option. If you want to eliminate eggs altogether, there's a product called Ener-G Egg Replacer that has worked well in all the breads we've tested. It's sold in health food stores or can be ordered directly from Ener-G (see Sources, page 189).

• Avoid such high-fat extras as nuts, cheese, sunflower seeds, bacon, cream cheese, and diced meats.

How to Reduce or Eliminate Sugar in Bread
❖❖❖

• Some sweeteners have more sweetening power than granulated sugar, which means you can use less of them. These include: honey, fructose, barley malt syrup, maple syrup, and maple sugar. They also contain more nutrients than table sugar.

• Puréed fruits and frozen fruit concentrates offer a more acceptable alternative to refined sugar for some people. Reduce the liquids in the recipe by the amount of fruit added.

• There's also a product called Fruit Sweet (see Sources, page 189), which is free of any refined sugars. It is a liquid blend of concentrated pear, peach, and pineapple juices. We've noticed a similar product called Fruit Source at our health food store. It's a combination of grape juice concentrate and whole rice syrup. When using either of these to replace granulated sugar, reduce the liquid in the recipe by an equal amount.

• Commercial fructose is usually refined from table sugar or corn syrup, not fruit. Natural sources for fructose are fruits, vegetables, and honey.

• Barley malt syrup is a complex sugar made from sprouted barley. It falls somewhere between honey and molasses in flavor. It's comprised of 77% maltose, 15% glucose, 7% sucrose, and 1% fructose. When we used it as a substitute for honey, our results were best when we used half the amount. If the recipe called for 2 tablespoons honey, we used 1 tablespoon barley malt syrup.

• Similar to barley malt syrup is brown rice syrup, a product of fermented brown rice.

• There are a wide variety of sugar substitutes on the market but the only ones that will withstand the heat of baking without turning bitter are Sugar Twin and Sunette's Sweet One. Nutrasweet has developed an encapsulated form that slowly releases its sweetener during cooking. The FDA is considering approval right now.

• Sugar Twin contains 1½ calories per teaspoon and its ingredients include dextrose, sodium, and saccharin. It comes in both brown and white "sugar" versions. Loaves tested with Sugar Twin using their suggested amounts proved to be much sweeter than we preferred. We suggest you experiment, too. We found that cutting the amount of sweetener in half produced a much more acceptable loaf for our palates.

• Sunette's Sweet One contains 2 calories per teaspoon and its ingredient list includes dextrose, acesulfame K, and cream of tartar. Our test samples using Sweet One didn't seem overly sweet. Their suggested sugar equivalents worked well.

• To eliminate adding any sugar to your recipes, use diastatic malt powder instead. (See our Sources section on page 189 if you have trouble locating it.) It contains active enzymes extracted from sprouted barley that will convert some of the flour's starch into maltose, supplying the necessary sugar the yeast needs to thrive and multiply.

• Avoid adding extra sugars unwittingly by the use of such products as chocolate chips, jams, marmalade, some peanut butters, sweetened condensed milk, dates, etc.

• Diabetics should check with their doctors for information on the beneficial effects of a high-fiber diet. Studies have shown it slows down the absorption of carbohydrates into the system.

Cutting the Salt in Half
✦✦✦

• Salt has an important role in bread baking: It inhibits the yeast's growth, strengthens the gluten, and brings out the wonderful flavors of the various ingredients. Omitting it altogether results in loaves that collapse during baking or never rise well to begin with; and in both cases they're very flat-tasting breads.

• It's easy to reduce the salt in most recipes; just a little experimenting on your part is needed. Start by reducing the amount in your recipe by ¼ teaspoon. If it's still an acceptable-looking loaf, next time try reducing the salt by another ¼ teaspoon.

• Items high in sodium include: cheese, salted butter, margarine, bacon, ham, salami, pepperoni, pickles, V-8 and tomato juice, peanuts, salted sunflower seeds, softened water, and processed foods. If you want to keep the sodium count in your breads at a low level, avoid adding these ingredients to your dough.

• Any "lite" salt or salt substitute must contain some sodium to perform effectively in your bread doughs. Just plain potassium chloride will not interact properly with the yeast and developing gluten. Understandably, we were unable to locate any salt substitutes listing sodium as an ingredient. Morton Lite Salt, however, contains both sodium and potassium chloride. It contains half the sodium of regular table salt. Loaves we tested using this lite salt as a replacement for the regular salt listed in the recipe were identical in size, shape, and texture to loaves baked with regular salt. (In case you're wondering, "Why even bother with the lite salt? Why not just reduce the salt in the recipe by 50 percent?" We tested many loaves and in most cases, the breads with the lite salt baked up better than those with half the amount of salt omitted.)

• Most of us should keep our sodium intake under 2,400 milligrams a day.

Lowering the Cholesterol in Your Bread
✦✦✦

• Animal fats equal cholesterol.

• To eliminate cholesterol in your daily bread, replace the animal fats such as butter, milk, egg yolks, sour cream, and cheese with healthier substitutions.

• Use nonfat milk rather than whole or lowfat milk.

• Select a buttermilk made with cultured nonfat milk rather than one made with lowfat milk.

• Use margarine instead of butter.

• Use vegetable oils such as canola, corn, soy, safflower, and olive oil to replace butter. (Canola oil is lower in saturated fats than any other oil.) Here is a comparison of the cholesterol and saturated fat content of most vegetable oils and shortenings:

	CHOLESTEROL	SATURATED FAT
Canola oil	0%	6%
Safflower oil	0%	9%
Sunflower oil	0%	11%
Corn oil	0%	13%
Peanut oil	0%	13%
Olive oil	0%	14%
Soybean oil	0%	15%
Cottonseed oil	0%	27%
Palm oil	0%	51%

Coconut oil	0%	77%
Margarine	0%	18%
Vegetable shortening	0%	26%
Butter	33%	54%

• Replace butter with an equal amount of puréed fruits, such as apple-sauce.

• Substitute two egg whites for one whole egg.

• Most liquid egg substitutes are cholesterol free. You can find them in your grocer's freezer or dairy section. For each large egg, substitute a scant ¼ cup liquid egg substitute.

• Replace each egg with Ener-G Egg Replacer or a scant ¼ cup water.

• Replace whole sour cream with fat-free sour cream.

• Most lowfat cottage cheeses and yogurts are low in cholesterol. Check the labels before purchasing.

High-fiber Breads
✦✦✦

• With the introduction of more and more processed and refined foods, fast foods, and high-sugar, high-fat snack foods, our consumption of fiber declined during the 1900s. Breads, cereals, beans, fruits, and vegetables—the best sources of dietary fiber—were pushed aside. It's exciting to think that the bread machine may stop or at least slow down this trend!

• Unlike vitamins, minerals, and protein, fiber isn't considered an essential nutrient, but many studies show a link between high-fiber diets and a reduction in certain types of diseases and cancers.

• High-fiber diets are lower in calories, more filling, and less likely to contribute to weight gain than diets low in fiber and high in protein.

• The recommended amount of fiber adults should consume daily is between 20 and 35 grams.

• There are two types of fiber—soluble and insoluble—and they perform two different functions in our systems.

• Soluble fiber absorbs water in the stomach and intestine, and thus provides a feeling of satiety and slows the absorption of food. This makes soluble fiber an ally in the battle of the bulge as well as an aid to persons with hypoglycemia and diabetes. Studies have also found that insoluble fiber lowers cholesterol and triglyceride levels in the blood.

• Soluble fiber dissolves in water. It is found mainly in fruits, vegetables, dried beans, peas, lentils, barley, and unrefined oats.

• Insoluble fiber passes through our systems pretty much intact and is known for its laxative effect.

• The best sources for insoluble fiber are wheat bran and whole grains. Dried beans, peas, fruits, and vegetables also contain some insoluble fiber.

• Eating a wide variety of fiber-rich foods is more beneficial than suddenly adding ten slices of whole wheat bread to your diet. It's better to include both types of fiber in your diet, rather than focus on one or the other.

• The whole-grain breads such as whole wheat, oatmeal, bran, cracked wheat, pumpernickel, and the fruit and vegetable breads are certainly an easy, delicious way to add extra fiber to your menus. Start gradually by replacing some of the high-fat, high-sugar foods with high-fiber ones. You'll eventually make a very painless, healthful change in your eating habits!

• If you want to increase the fiber in your breads, add ⅓ to ½ cup oatmeal, oat bran, bulgur, cooked cracked wheat, sprouted grains, miller's bran, or multigrain cereals to your breads. Observe your dough as it is kneading because you will probably have to add 1 to 2 tablespoons extra liquid as well.

• Diced, raw fruits or vegetables are also fiber-rich additions you can make to your daily bread. In that case, when you add fruits or vegetables, you'll need to either reduce the liquids in your bread or add some extra flour while it mixes.

Breads for Animal Lovers
❖❖❖

No, this segment isn't about creating special breads to take to the zoo or recipes for extra-special morsels to toss to the ducks and birds in your city park. The following helpful hints are meant for those of you with gentle spirits who choose to protect animals and their products rather than eat them. If you don't already know, it's possible, with just a few minor changes, to create wonderful breads that will suit your needs.

• When milk is used in a recipe, you can substitute an equal quantity of water, fruit juice, vegetable juice, or the water used for cooking vegetables or beans. (When using the liquid left after cooking beans, use no more than ½ cup or the result will be too rich.) There are also products made from soy or rice that are milk-like in consistency and appearance. They include: Vita Soy, Fat-free Soy Moo, Edensoy, West Soy, Rice Dream, and probably many others in different parts of the country. (Be a label reader; some milk-like beverages are much higher in fat than others.)

• If your breads with soy "milk" aren't turning out well, try boiling the liquid first then letting it cool before adding it to the rest of the ingredients. There may have been some bacteria that were meddling with the yeast and keeping it from doing its job.

• To replace nonfat dry milk powder in recipes, Ener-G Soy Quick, a powdered soy drink, worked beautifully in our test loaves. We saw other similar products in the health food stores such as: Fearn Soya Powder, Vitamite, and Better Than Milk. Ener-G's Nut Quick, an almond-based powdered beverage, caught our eye and is definitely on our long list of products to try in the future.

• As we've mentioned a few times, there's a product in the health food stores, also produced by Ener-G, called Egg Replacer. It's strictly a non-dairy, non-animal product made from ingredients such as potato starch, tapioca flour, and leavening. We've been very pleased with the results when substituting 2 teaspoons Egg Replacer plus 3 tablespoons water for each large egg in bread recipes. It even made a great "Egg" Bread!

• If you prefer not to use any commercially packaged egg replacement, you may simply omit the egg and replace it with a scant ¼ cup liquid.

• If you've already read through the long list of sugar substitutes in previous sections, you know that there are many ways to replace honey in bread recipes; probably the most closely related product is barley malt syrup. If you prefer not to use sugar at all, try diastatic malt powder. Using ¼ to ½ teaspoon in 1- and 1½-pound recipes respectively, produces the best results.

Wheat-free/Gluten-free Breads
❖❖❖

Until just a few months ago, if someone had asked us if it was possible to bake breads with 100% non-wheat and gluten-free flours, we would have replied, "No way!" Vital wheat gluten is just that: vital! We've been very pleasantly surprised to discover a small group of people on the Prodigy network who are doing "the impossible." They're baking breads all the time without that crucial ingredient. Most of them have, or bake for people who have, an intolerance for any foods containing wheat and/or gluten. If a bread contains even the smallest amount of wheat, rye, oats, barley, millet, buckwheat, or triticale, it's unacceptable. Consequently, baking an edible bread becomes a real challenge. Add to that the rigidly programmed cycles of most bread machines, and producing an acceptable loaf of gluten-free bread is an incredible feat!

It's our hope to explore this "phenomenon" more fully in the future and create new wheat-free/gluten-free bread recipes. (Gluten-free also means wheat-free, so those with wheat allergies can make good use of gluten-free recipes, too.) For the time being, we'd like to share some of the tried-and-true recipes and suggestions from a very unique group of men and women on Prodigy. They're proving that it's possible to have fresher, better-tasting breads at a fraction of the cost health food stores charge.

• Xanthan gum is the "glue" that binds the bread dough together and replaces the gluten in these breads. It is a powder derived from a laboratory-grown organism called *xanthomonas compestris.* Most 1½-pound loaves use about 3½ teaspoons xanthan gum.

• Take it from two who learned the hard way, if you spill xanthan gum on the floor or countertop, you're better off vacuuming it up or brushing it into the sink with a dry towel than trying to clean it up with a wet cloth or sponge. Once wet, it becomes very gooey and a major headache to remove.

• Two other "gluten replacers" are guar gum and methylcellulose (methocel). Ener-G Foods (see Sources, page 189) stocks all three.

• Gluten-free ingredients for breads include: white rice flour (coarse), white rice flour (fine), brown rice flour, sweet rice flour, rice bran, rice starch, rice polish, tapioca flour, tapioca starch, potato flour, potato starch flour, soy flour, yellow corn flour, white corn flour, yellow cornmeal, white cornmeal, polenta meal, cornstarch, corn bran, and acorn flour. There are also several flours made from such legumes as peas, mung beans, lentils, and garbanzo beans. The options are quite amazing, and are available at most health food stores. Others are available from sources listed in the back of this book (see page 189). The rest can be hand-milled.

• In addition to the above flours, Ener-G sells packaged gluten-free bread machine mixes. Experiment a little by adding chopped, dried fruits or herbs and spices to them for variety.

• Observe your bread dough during the first kneading cycle. If the machine has difficulty mixing the dough thoroughly, use a spatula carefully to assist it once or twice.

• Gluten-free bread dough does not form a smooth ball as does wheat flour dough. It more closely resembles whipped potatoes and doesn't always mix up well in the bread machine unless you watch it and assist it occasionally with a rubber spatula. We had more success by reversing the normal order of adding ingredients. Start with the yeast and dry ingredients, add half the wet ingredients, then press Start. Allow the ingredients to mix for a minute or so, then gradually add the rest of the liquids.

• Beat eggs well before adding them to the rest of the ingredients.

• Bread machines with a dough pin seemed to do the best job of mixing gluten-free breads.

• The Celiac Spruce Association/USA, Inc., is a national support organization that offers information and referral services. They have published a series of low-cost brochures on the gluten-free diet, gluten-free commercial foods, and related topics. They also offer a newsletter as part of their annual membership fee. For information, you can call them from 10 A.M. to noon and from 1 to 3 P.M. Central time at 1-402-558-0600, or write to them: CSA/USA, Inc., P.O. Box 31700, Omaha, NE 68131-0700.

GENE'S BASIC RICE BREAD
✦✦✦

Gene Hill, who lives in Davis, California, bakes this bread at least twice a week. He recommends trying it as a toasted cheese sandwich. Grill it with thin slices of red onion or bell pepper and cheese.

1 cup fresh gluten-free
   buttermilk
¼ cup butter, melted
1 teaspoon rice vinegar
1½ teaspoons salt
2 cups brown rice flour
⅓ cup potato starch flour
⅓ cup tapioca flour

¼ cup sugar
3½ teaspoons xanthan gum
3 eggs
½ cup water (for Welbilt/DAK
   and Zojirushi machines, add 2
   tablespoons more water)
1½ tablespoons active dry
   yeast

1. Place the buttermilk, melted butter, rice vinegar, and salt in bread pan. Stir with a rubber spatula.

2. In a large bowl, combine all the dry ingredients except the yeast. Mix well with a whisk.

3. In a separate bowl, combine the eggs and water; beat lightly.

4. Place ½ of the dry ingredients in the bread pan. Add the egg mixture. Add the remainder of the dry ingredients; sprinkle the yeast on top. Select Light Crust setting and press Start.

5. Observe the dough frequently during the kneading cycles. If it does not appear to be mixing well, use a rubber spatula to assist it occasionally.

6. After the baking cycle ends, remove bread from pan, place on wire rack, and allow to cool 1 hour before slicing.

VARIATIONS:

• You can substitute olive oil for the butter.

• Replace ¼ to ½ cup of the rice flour with another gluten-free flour, such as yellow or blue corn flour, polenta meal, or soy flour.

• You can add at least ¼ cup grated cheddar cheese for a new flavor.

• Sauté some onions in the melted butter, allow them to cool, then add them and your favorite herbs to create an onion/herb bread.

```
CRUST: LIGHT
OPTIONAL BAKE CYCLE:
   SWEET BREAD
   RAPID BAKE
```

BOB'S CHEDDAR CHEESE BREAD

❖❖❖

This rich bread is flecked with grated cheese. If you're daring, try adding 2 or 3 tablespoons of diced jalapeño peppers to it. It's also good toasted. We have Bob and Melody Gabriel to thank for sharing this gluten-free recipe.

1½-POUND	1-POUND
2¼ teaspoons (1 packet) active dry yeast	2 teaspoons active dry yeast
1 cup brown rice flour	1 cup brown rice flour
2 cups white rice flour	1½ cups white rice flour
3½ teaspoons xanthan gum	2 teaspoons xanthan gum
2 tablespoons sugar	1½ tablespoons sugar
1 teaspoon salt	¾ teaspoon salt
1½ cups (6 ounces) grated extra-sharp Cheddar cheese	1¼ cups (5 ounces) grated extra-sharp Cheddar cheese
¼ cup nonfat dry milk powder	3 tablespoons nonfat dry milk powder
2 tablespoons butter or margarine, softened	1¾ tablespoons butter or margarine, softened
2 large eggs, well beaten	1 extra large or jumbo egg, well beaten
1¼ cups warm water	1⅓ cups warm water

1. Place all ingredients, except the warm water, in bread pan, select Light Crust setting, and press Start. While the machine is kneading, gradually pour in the water. If the dough does not mix well, use a rubber spatula to assist it occasionally.

2. After the baking cycle ends, remove bread from pan, place on wire rack, and allow to cool 1 hour before slicing.

```
CRUST: LIGHT
OPTIONAL BAKE CYCLES:
   SWEET BREAD
   RAPID BAKE
```

MELODY'S BROWN AND WHITE BREAD
❖❖❖

Melody Gabriel from Vero Beach, Florida, shared this basic, easy-to-make recipe and when others tried it, the consensus was "Wonderful!"

1½-POUND	1-POUND
2¼ teaspoons (1 packet) active dry yeast	2 teaspoons active dry yeast
1 cup brown rice flour	1 cup brown rice flour
2 cups white rice flour	1½ cups white rice flour
3½ teaspoons xanthan gum	2¾ teaspoons xanthan gum
¼ cup plus 2 teaspoons sugar	2 tablespoons sugar
1½ teaspoons salt	1 teaspoon salt
1⅓ cups nonfat dry milk powder	1 cup nonfat dry milk powder
¼ cup butter or margarine, melted	1 tablespoon butter or margarine, melted
2 large eggs, well beaten	1 extra large or jumbo egg, well beaten
1¾ cups warm water	1⅓ cups warm water

1. Place all ingredients, except the warm water, in bread pan and press Start. While the machine is kneading, gradually pour in the water. If the dough does not mix well, use a rubber spatula to assist it occasionally.

2. After the baking cycle ends, remove bread from pan, place on wire rack, and allow to cool 1 hour before slicing.

```
CRUST: MEDIUM
OPTIONAL BAKE CYCLES:
   SWEET BREAD
   RAPID BAKE
```

✦✦✦ 5 ✦✦✦

Helpful Hints and Troubleshooting Techniques

Tips for Baking the Perfect Loaf
✦✦✦

PRIOR TO BAKING

• Within a week, most new owners realize that their bread machine is one of those rarities . . . a kitchen appliance that will remain on the countertop and be used constantly; it will not be relegated to some back corner of the pantry. If you can manage it, you will save time by storing all your bread-baking items in one area. We find it convenient to have small containers and jars of flour, sugar, brown sugar, nonfat dry milk, oats, oil, honey, molasses, salt, raisins, potato flakes, cornmeal, herbs, spices, and measuring utensils all within an arm's reach.

• Store your whole-grain flours, wheat germ, bran, nuts, and seeds (including sesame and poppy seeds) in the refrigerator or freezer. It's helpful to have a second freezer.

BAKING GREAT BREAD

• For the best breads, use the freshest ingredients.

• If your well-used bread pan seems to have lost its nonstick ability, spraying it lightly with a nonstick cooking spray before adding ingredients will ease the process of removing the baked bread later on.

• Learn to judge the dough as we discussed in the Essential Guidelines for Bread Machine Baking (page 43). It's a small step you can take when making a bread for the first time that will often prevent disappointing results four hours later.

• Use large eggs unless the recipe states otherwise.

• Use room-temperature ingredients for best results unless your instruction booklet says otherwise. Liquids should be heated to 80°F.

• Use a dry measuring cup to measure the dry ingredients and a glass or plastic liquid measuring cup to measure the liquids.

• Avoid answering or talking on the phone while trying to measure ingredients for your next bread. We've ruined many loaves that way!

• We find it helpful to collect all the ingredients on the counter before adding them one by one to the bread pan; there seems to be less chance of omitting one of them. Yeast bread made without yeast is a monstrosity even the family pet will snub.

• Follow your manufacturer's directions as to the order in which you place the ingredients into the bread pan. However, unless your machine has a yeast dispenser that separates the yeast from the liquid ingredients, when using the Delayed Bake timer we recommend adding the liquids first and the yeast last. Making a well in the dry ingredients for the yeast prevents it from coming in contact with the liquids too soon.

• The more ingredients you add to your dough, the heavier it will be. If it's a reluctant riser, you will have to either reduce the amount of additions or give the dough a boost with an enhancer such as extra gluten, ascorbic acid, or a commercial dough enhancer.

• Exceeding ¼ and ⅓ cup of fat and/or sugar in 1- and 1½-pound loaves respectively, will effectively destroy the gluten's chances to expand. You'll be left with a very compact, mini loaf.

• When using butter straight from the refrigerator, cut it into small pieces or soften it first in the microwave.

- Any time you add more than 2 tablespoons of butter or margarine to a recipe, cut the shortening into smaller pieces first.

- Whole-grain breads will not rise as high as breads made with all-white bread flour.

- If you want to use ingredients, such as Grape Nuts or granola, that have the potential to scratch the coated surface of your bread pan, add them with the liquids and let them soak several minutes to soften.

- Gluten absorbs water, so doughs with low-gluten flours will be stickier during kneading than wheat flour doughs.

- Select the Light Crust setting when baking breads that are high in fat or sugar, or contain cheese, eggs, or whole-grain flours.

- When cooking or roasting any ingredients, be sure to let them cool to room temperature before adding them to the rest of the ingredients.

- To get the last little bit of honey or molasses out of the jar, warm it for 5 to 10 seconds in the microwave.

- It pays to peek at the dough near the end of its rising period. If it is threatening to overflow the pan, simply deflate it slightly by poking it once or twice with a toothpick.

USING THE DOUGH CYCLE; BAKING BREADS IN THE OVEN

- If you prefer to make a bread on the dough cycle then bake it in the oven, turn it out onto a floured or lightly oiled countertop, shape it into a loaf, and place it in a greased 9 × 5 inch loaf pan (for the 1½-pound dough) or an 8½ × 4½ inch pan (for the 1-pound dough). In the case of a French bread or country rye, you can shape it into a free-form oblong or round loaf and place it on a greased baking sheet. Cover the shaped loaf and let rise in a warm place until doubled, 30 to 45 minutes, then bake. You can bake most loaves at 375°F for 35 to 45 minutes.

- To create a warm environment for rising doughs that you plan to bake outside the machine, turn on your oven to the lowest setting (Warm) for one minute, then turn it off, and place the covered dough in the warm oven to rise.

- Do not cover rising doughs with terrycloth towels. They become imbedded in the dough.

- When baking breads in the oven instead of the bread machine, darker pans will produce darker crusts. If you choose a glass loaf pan, reduce the oven temperature by 25°F.

THE RAISIN/NUT CYCLE

• When the machine beeps to add extras such as raisins, nuts, or dried fruits, avoid tossing the raisins and dried fruits into the bread pan all clumped together. They may not separate properly by the time the kneading cycle ends.

• Dusting the raisins and dried fruits with a little flour or cinnamon first will help them separate and mix into the dough.

• If you want a different flavor, while the dough is mixing, soak your raisins in some inexpensive vanilla, brandy, or rum. When the machine beeps to add extra ingredients, drain them well, then add.

• If you have no raisin/nut cycle or don't want to use it, try refrigerating or freezing your raisins, chopped dried fruits, and nuts. They hold their shape better and don't break down quite as easily. If you choose to freeze them, spread them out on a cookie sheet and place the sheet in the freezer. Once the separate pieces are frozen, you can place them in a heavy-duty plastic bag or container for longer storage.

• If your machine does not have a raisin/nut cycle and the ingredients added at the start are pulverized by the end of the second kneading cycle, you can set a timer to coincide with the last ten minutes of your second kneading cycle. If you find that they're not being fully incorporated into the dough, then try adding them at the beginning of the second kneading cycle.

• If you constantly miss the signal to add ingredients because your machine has a very soft "beep" or because you're not in the kitchen at the time, set a louder timer or carry one with you. Some gourmet kitchen stores and mail-order catalogs sell a small timer that you can wear like a necklace. This would be ideal. It's also a handy way of reminding yourself to check the dough every so often when trying a new recipe, if you tend to get busy with other projects.

AFTER THE BREAD IS BAKED

• If you have difficulty removing a bread from the pan, rap the corner of the bread pan on a wooden cutting board or padded surface several times. Avoid sticking a knife or metal spatula into the pan to release it; you'll scratch the coating.

• A good serrated bread knife is invaluable. If you're not pleased with your slicing skills, we've found that an electric knife helps produce more uniform slices. And if all else fails, there are some very compact electric food slicers that will produce perfect slices every time! You'll find them in kitchen specialty stores and catalogs.

• We know . . . it's oh, so tempting to cut into that freshly baked loaf of bread the moment you turn it out of the bread pan. Try to wait at least 15 minutes to give it a chance to set up enough to be sliceable. A hot loaf of bread will collapse or compress if you try to slice it too soon.

• Some breads bake up much softer than others. If you can, wait until the next day to slice those softies.

• Get in the habit of keeping all the little pieces and parts of your bread pan together. A mixing blade lost down the disposal can mean *weeks* without homemade bread (and probably without a disposal)! If you know yourself well and see this one coming, you'd be wise to order a spare or two right now while you're thinking about it.

S.O.S.

• If you run into a problem you can't solve and that we haven't covered in this book, there are many people available to lend a hand. If it has to do with an ingredient, many companies have 800 numbers you can call. Look on the package or call 1-800-555-1212 for 800 information. If it's related to your machine, call the manufacturer and ask for customer service. We've found that many bread machine manufacturers have helpful, courteous people available to assist you. Keep in mind that they're also extremely busy. Have the facts and the model number of your machine at hand before dialing.

• We'd be remiss if we didn't mention our favorite source of friendly assistance, new ideas, and consumer feedback: the multitude of computer bulletin boards with food-related topics. A bulletin board is a central point of contact where computer users meet to gather and share information. Most bulletin boards are easily accessible if you have a home computer, a modem, and telecommunications software to drive it. The best-known commercial boards are Compuserve, Prodigy, GEnie, America Online, and National Videotex. If you're interested in joining one of the major Bulletin Board Networks, it's well worth your while to compare prices and services first. You can run up a substantial bill each month if the service you join doesn't offer off-line message reading and/or free (or discounted) access to their bulletin boards between certain hours. Also, verify that their connection is a local phone number for you. The monthly membership fees vary widely, too. To avoid the hefty monthly bills altogether, join one of the noncommercial Bulletin Board Systems that you can access locally. They offer a variety of networks—Fidonet and Internet to name just two—that carry cooking-related conferences such as The Cooking Echo (on Fidonet). If you're interested but not a computer maven, call a friend or several of the computer stores in your area until you hook up with someone who is willing to answer your questions and help you locate a suitable Bulletin Board Service. We can't recommend these bulletin boards highly enough. They're a fabulous way to exchange ideas and recipes, get help, learn about the different types of bread machines, and meet some wonderful people. Your knowledge of bread machine baking will grow exponentially once you jump in and begin sharing your experiences and reading what others have learned. Linda is currently a member of several bulletin boards and can vouch that bread machine baking is one HOT topic!

How to Adapt Your Favorite Recipes for the Bread Machine
❖❖❖

Once you're familiar with your machine and glowing with confidence because of all the "masterpieces" you've baked up, you'll probably want to branch out creatively. Wonderful childhood memories will slowly trickle back into your consciousness: Aunt Loretta's famous yeast rolls that you could never get enough of, the dark pungent breads your grandmother learned to bake in "the old country," or the incomparable Jewish rye breads from the corner deli. With the original recipe in hand or a reasonable facsimile you've found in a cookbook, you can duplicate those treasures. Here are some guidelines:

• First, you will have to reduce the volume of your original recipe to fit the flour and liquid capacities of your bread machine. You'll find that most recipes will have to be reduced by half or two-thirds to suit your machine.

• Once you reduce your recipe, the quantities of the essential ingredients should fall within the following parameters. Make minor adjustments if necessary.

1½-POUND LOAF	1-POUND LOAF
1⅛ to 1¼ cups liquid	⅞ to 1 cup liquid
3 to 4 cups flour*	2 to 2⅔ cups flour*
½ to 1½ teaspoons salt	¼ to 1 teaspoon salt
1 to 4 tablespoons fat	2 teaspoons to 3 tablespoons fat
1 to 4 tablespoons sweetener	2 teaspoons to 3 tablespoons sweetener
1½ to 3 teaspoons active dry yeast	1½ to 3 teaspoons active dry yeast

*Whole-grain breads often require the larger amounts of flour to produce an acceptable-size loaf. You will probably have to increase the amount of liquid as well when using the extra flour.

• If your recipe reductions result in odd measurements such as ⅓ teaspoon cinnamon, you have a few options: You can approximate a ⅓ teaspoon measure by using a heaping ¼ teaspoon of the ingredient, or you can choose to add ¼ teaspoon or ½ teaspoon of the spice, according to your taste. Don't worry too much about fractional amounts of seasonings, etc.; it's the liquid, flour, and salt that are the crucial ingredients. Care should be taken to measure them accurately.

• One large egg equals a scant ¼ cup (4 tablespoons) liquid. If the original recipe, which you reduced by half, listed one egg, you can use either 2 tablespoons of liquid egg substitute to equal that ½ egg or add the entire egg but reduce the liquid in the recipe by the extra 2 tablespoons liquid in the whole egg.

• A word of advice: We've found ratios of 2:1, 2½:1, and 3:1 cups of wheat flour to cups of non-wheat flour work best in our bread machines. If your recipe is 100% whole grain with little or no wheat flour, you will need to adjust the proportions to include a minimum of two cups of wheat flour for each cup of non-wheat flour to avoid creating a loaf that would break your foot if you dropped it.

• If you're recreating a roll recipe or a specialty-type bread using the dough cycle, the dough is usually easier to handle if you reduce the liquid by 2 tablespoons. However, if this is too stiff a dough for your machine and it sounds like it's struggling to mix it, return the 2 tablespoons of liquid to the dough.

• When adapting a recipe for use in the bread machine, you should monitor it closely the first time you bake it. Jot down any adjustments you make to the dough during the kneading cycle. Observe the dough as it rises. If it rises too tall that first time, you'll know to reduce the liquid, yeast, or sugar or increase the amount of salt in the future.

• If, after several attempts to duplicate a favorite recipe, you end up with a great-tasting bread that refuses to bake up properly in the machine, don't give up on it. In the future, make it on the dough cycle, remove it from the machine, shape it, allow it to rise until doubled, then bake it in the oven!

The Next Step:
How to Create Your Own Recipes
❖❖❖

If you've adapted several of your favorite recipes successfully, the next step is to try your hand at creating a few of your own. With the following guidelines, you should be able to develop a one-of-a-kind masterpiece that will make you proud!

• For a starting point, refer to the generic 1- and 1½-pound recipes on page 106.

• Use a minimum of ⅜ cup of liquid for each cup of flour. We found it easier to start with a dry dough and add liquid when necessary during the kneading cycle than to try and correct an overly wet dough.

• If you choose to include "wet" ingredients such as sour cream, cottage cheese, yogurt, mashed potatoes, fruits, and vegetables, you must consider them as part of your liquids. As a general rule of thumb, regard them as half liquid and deduct that amount of liquid from your basic recipe. Adding ½ cup of chopped onions means reducing the liquid in your recipe by ¼ cup. Watch the bread dough while it is kneading. If it looks too wet or too dry, add flour or water as needed, 1 tablespoon at a time.

• When using eggs in your recipe, calculate each large egg as the equivalent of a scant ¼ cup of liquid.

• Keep in mind that the more you add beyond the basics of flour, liquid, sugar, salt, fat, and yeast, the heavier the bread will be and the longer it will take to rise. Limit them to roughly ¼ of your total flour; i.e., ½ cup of extras for 2 cups of flour, ¾ cup of extras for 3 cups of flour. Extras include items such as: dried fruits, nuts, seeds, whole grains, and raisins.

• We found ratios of 2:1, 2½:1, and 3:1 cups of wheat flour to cups of non-wheat flour to work best in our bread machines. For instance, if you want to create a rye bread, experiment using 1 cup of rye flour and 2, 2½, or 3 cups of wheat flour (that can be a mixture of white and whole wheat). For the smaller 1-pound machine a 3:1 ratio would mean ½ cup rye flour and 1½ cups wheat flour.

• Start with ½ teaspoon of salt per cup of flour; in some cases you will be able to reduce that amount, even by as much as half. But don't try to omit it altogether. Salt is critical to the success of the bread.

• Most loaves don't need more than ½ tablespoon fat per cup of flour.

• The average amount of sugar per cup of flour is ½ tablespoon.

• Do not add more than ¼ cup of either butter or sugar to any 1-pound recipe or more than ⅓ cup of either to 1½-pound recipes.

- Yeast amounts vary according to brand and type. Most loaves need a minimum of 1½ teaspoons active dry yeast. Use ½ teaspoon instant or fast-rising yeast per cup of flour if you plan to bake the loaf on the Regular cycle and double that amount if you plan to bake it on the Rapid Bake cycle.

- Watch the dough closely during both kneading cycles. After several minutes of kneading, if it looks too dry or too wet, make the proper adjustments. By the end of the second kneading cycle, it should form a smooth, slightly tacky-to-the-touch ball of dough.

- It pays to observe and take notes each time you attempt a new bread.

- When you make corrections to a recipe, try to limit them to one change at a time. Often times simply adjusting the amount of liquid will make all the difference you really need. If you increase the yeast, decrease the salt, and increase the sugar at the same time, you'll never know which change was the effective one.

- Don't get too discouraged if your first efforts aren't stellar successes. Most "blue-ribbon" breads take several attempts before perfection is achieved.

- By all means, let your creative juices flow! Once you start concocting your own bread recipes, trips to the grocery and health food store can be an adventure. Have fun . . . pick something new each time to incorporate into your next creation.

Home Milling
+++

If you want to take homemade, healthy bread baking to new heights, the next step is to purchase a manual or electric grain mill. Once you try breads made from grains you grind into flour yourself, you may never return to commercially milled whole-grain flours! Freshly milled wheat is much sweeter than store-bought whole wheat flour, which can often have a bitter undertaste. We recommend using freshly milled wheat in a very simple, low-sugar recipe to capture its naturally sweet essence and delicate richness.

Freshly ground whole-grains will turn rancid rather quickly so grind up only what you plan to use. (The whole-grain kernels will keep at room temperature indefinitely.) We've found that 1 cup of wheat berries produces a scant 1¾ cups flour. One pound of wheat berries equals approximately 4½ cups of flour. We wish we could also tell you the calories burnt per minute when you grind it manually but so far we haven't seen that listed on any exercise chart! It should be; it's a bit of a workout. We think it's comparable to chopping your own wood for the evening fire . . . the fire burns just that much warmer; the bread tastes just that much sweeter.

We've listed several sources (see page 189) for mills and whole grains. When you're in the market for a grain mill, ask questions based on your intended usage and look for one that is easy to take apart and thoroughly clean. We also found that we could purchase 50-pound sacks of hard, red, winter wheat berries from local health food stores. Ask the manager. They may be willing to discount the price, too.

Depending on your type of mill, there's a wide variety of grains, beans, seeds, and nuts you can grind into flour for your breads: wheat, rye, corn, rice, barley, oats, buckwheat, millet, kamut, quinoa, peas, mung beans, garbanzos, and lentils for starters. We've even heard of acorn flour, but you might have to fight the little chipmunks and squirrels for them. Let loose your imagination . . . just think of all the delicious, new breads you can concoct. So come on . . . let's get cranking!

How to Counteract
Troublesome Climatic Conditions
✦✦✦

There's no getting around it . . . the weather has a definite effect on your bread. When you bake a particular loaf day after day with varying results, changes in the weather are often the cause. When it's humid, the flour will be more moist than usual and won't absorb as much of the liquids you add. If you use the amount of liquid the recipe calls for, your doughs will often be too wet and bake up with a course, holey texture. Conversely, when it is extremely dry outside, your flour will be very "thirsty" and, without adjustments, the baked bread will be heavy and dry. Here's what you can do to work with Mother Nature:

• On humid days, decrease the liquid in the recipe by 2 tablespoons. Watch the dough as it mixes. If you think it needs just a little more moisture, add liquid a teaspoon at a time. As it nears the end of the second kneading cycle, it should be a smooth, pliable, slightly tacky ball of dough.

• When the weather is dry, observe your dough during the kneading cycle. If you think it looks dry, add extra liquid a teaspoon at a time until it forms that silky smooth ball.

• Some people who live in very humid or dry climates find it more accurate to weigh rather than measure the flour. If you choose to do so, the helpful people at General Mills (Gold Medal flour) informed us that 1 cup of all-purpose flour weighs 4.59 ounces (130 grams), 1 cup bread flour weighs 4.76 ounces (135 grams), and 1 cup whole wheat flour weighs 4.51 ounces (128 grams).

• During the cold winter months, extra care has to be taken to keep your machine away from cold exterior walls, chilly windows, and cold drafts. It's time to move the bread machine out of the cold laundry room or garage into a warmer room in the house. If you normally don't warm your liquids during the rest of the year, you may have to do so on exceptionally cold days.

• Summer means heat and that can bring its own problems. Doughs tend to rise faster and higher when it's warm in the house. It can mean that normally tall breads will suddenly overflow the pan or collapse during baking. To cool the dough, start with refrigerated ingredients and cold liquids or choose a cooler time of day to bake. Also, during those hot summer days, keep the bread machine out of drafts caused by air-conditioning or ceiling fans.

Adjustments for High-altitude Bread Baking
✜✜✜

If you're a bread machine owner and live 7,000 feet or more above sea level, you may be experiencing some sunken loaves. At higher elevations, the dough "overproofs." Due to the lower barometric pressure at high altitudes, the carbon dioxide gas bubbles created by the yeast expand more rapidly. Therefore, the bread rises too high, the gluten loses its strength, and the bread collapses during baking. Take heart, it's an easy problem to correct. No need to pack up your bread machine and move down to the flatlands. Try the following combination of suggestions:

• Reduce the amount of yeast by about ⅓. This will create less carbon dioxide and the bread will not rise as quickly.

• Increase the salt by 25 percent. This will have the same effect as decreasing the yeast. The bread will rise slower and be less likely to sink during baking.

• Add from ½ to 1 tablespoon gluten per cup of flour. Increasing the gluten will give added strength to your bread.

• Watch your dough as it mixes. You may need to add at least 1 to 3 tablespoons more liquid since flour stored at high altitudes tends to be drier than that stored below 7,000 feet.

(These recommended alterations were shared by Irwin Franzel, a friend and very knowledgeable bread machine baker. With his "Zoji" S-15 under one arm and bread-baking supplies under the other, he took off for a Colorado vacation and baked up numerous loaves of "high-altitude" bread. By adjusting the salt, gluten, yeast, and liquid, he was finally able to produce consistently well-shaped breads.)

• Two other options: Because of the rapid-rising nature of high-altitude breads, try baking them on the Rapid Bake cycle of your machine to reduce the rising time. If your machine has a programmable mode, watch the loaf as it rises; when it nears the top of the bread pan, switch to the Bake cycle manually.

Small Loaves:
A Multitude of Causes and the Solutions
❖❖❖

We've observed that the most common problem faced by bread machine owners is bread that fails to rise properly. As you can see from the following list, there are any number of reasons why that happens as frequently as it does. We've started with the most common causes and listed the rest in an approximate order of their occurrence.

By the way, if you're having problems with a bread not rising properly, we suggest you make only one change at a time when you're trying to correct the problem. That way, you'll be able to clearly identify the correction(s) that works.

- *Were you baking a 100% whole wheat bread?*

Whole wheat breads will normally not rise as high as white flour breads. The bran and wheat germ they contain make the flour heavier than white flour. To give it a boost, add 1 tablespoon gluten per cup of flour or replace part of the whole wheat flour with white bread flour.

- *Were you baking a whole-grain bread that had a very low proportion of wheat flour to non-wheat flour?*

In all the breads we've tested, the best results were achieved by using a minimum of 2 cups wheat flour for every cup of non-wheat flour.

- *Was the bread dough dry and very stiff as it was kneading?*

Next time, as it kneads, add more liquid 1 tablespoon at a time until the dough forms a silky-smooth, pliable ball of dough.

- *Were there too many "heavy" extras such as raisins, bran, whole grains, seeds, or nuts?*

The more you add to the basic dough, the more it will weigh it down and make it harder to rise. Limit those extras to ¼ cup per cup of flour.

- *Did you use a stone-ground or coarse hand-milled whole-grain flour?*

The gluten in coarse-textured flour does not develop as well as the gluten in finely milled flours. You may have to use a dough enhancer to increase the height of your next loaves.

- *Is your tap water very hard?*

To counteract it and create a more yeast-friendly acidic environment, add 1 teaspoon lemon juice or vinegar to the water.

- *Did you use all-purpose flour rather than bread flour?*

The difference in gluten content between the two flours can make a significant difference in the height of your bread.

- *Did you bake the bread on a Rapid Bake cycle?*

Many times our test loaves baked on the Rapid Bake cycle were up to one inch smaller than those baked on the Regular cycle. In addition, not all loaves bake up well on the faster cycle, especially those that are high in fat or laden with extras.

- *Has your yeast lost its vitality?*

Refer to page 68 for directions on how to test your yeast's activity.

- *What brand of yeast did you use?*

We've found that different brands of yeast vary in their effectiveness in the bread machine. We recommend Red Star yeast.

- *Are you a "flour scooper"?*

Scooping the flour out of the bag or canister will result in adding much more flour to the dough than the recipe calls for. Measure the flour by lightly spooning it into the measuring cup then leveling it off.

- *Were most of your ingredients taken from the refrigerator or freezer?*

Doughs created with room-temperature ingredients produce the best breads. Try to plan ahead and remove ingredients from the fridge or freezer at least one half hour in advance. If this isn't possible, set your bread on a Delayed Bake timer and allow it to sit at room temperature for at least one half hour before starting.

- *If your machine has a Preheat cycle, did you place the bread pan in the machine and press Start immediately?*

If you have a machine with a Preheat cycle that warms the ingredients before mixing, you should wait at least 30 seconds before pressing Start to give the sensor time to register the cold ingredients. Also, keep the sensor and the bottom of the pan clean and lint free.

- *Were your liquids too hot?*

Start with liquids at 80°F (approximately room temperature). If they're too hot, they will kill the yeast.

- *Were your liquids too cold?*

If you used liquids straight from the refrigerator and your machine doesn't have a Preheat cycle, they were too cold for the yeast to activate properly.

- *Did you add more salt or salty ingredients to the recipe?*

Salt inhibits the yeast's growth. If you want to add salty ingredients, reduce the salt amount listed in the recipe.

- *Did you omit the sugar accidentally or on purpose?*

We've been able to bake some breads without sugar or any of its substitutes but not 100 percent of the time. The sweetener is usually an essential ingredient. If you choose to bake breads without it, try Sweet One, Sugar Twin, or diastatic malt powder.

- *Did you forget to add the yeast?*

If this was the cause of your small loaf, you'll know it . . . it just never rose. Place all your ingredients out on the counter before you begin measuring from now on.

- *Did you dump the yeast into the bread pan right on top of the salt?*

Salt and yeast don't mix. A high concentration of salt can kill the yeast if they come in contact with one another.

• *Did you forget to install the mixing blade?*

It's amazing how often this happens! Get in the habit of checking the dough as it begins to mix and you'll catch this in time to correct it. (Sticking your hand into that goop and blindly fumbling around to line up the post and the blade correctly will be an experience you won't soon forget!)

• *Are you experiencing an extreme weather condition: is it either very humid or incredibly dry?*

If it's very humid, start by decreasing the liquid in the recipe by 2 tablespoons; adjust as needed while the dough is mixing. If the air is very dry, you may have to add liquid as the dough is kneading.

• *Do you find in the wintertime that your breads are smaller?*

When it's cold, move your bread machine to a warm location. Avoid putting it near cold exterior walls, chilly windows, or in a draft. Turn up the heater if your home is especially chilly.

• *Did the mixing blade fail to function properly?*

Make sure it's pushed all the way down onto the post before you begin adding ingredients.

• *Did the dough fail to mix well?*

Make sure the bread pan is seated correctly in the machine; push it in until it clicks into place. (Or, in some machines, rotate it until you feel it lock into place and it won't lift out.)

• *Is your machine not kneading the dough as well as it used to; consequently, the gluten isn't being fully developed?*

It's possible the belt is stretched or slipping. Take your bread machine to a dependable appliance repair store that can replace the belt for you.

• *Was there any soap residue left in the bread pan after washing?*

Traces of soap will interfere with the yeast. Make sure you rinse your bread pan well after washing it.

• *Were you interrupted by a phone call in the middle of measuring your ingredients?*

It's possible you omitted or mismeasured something. Try again. Send the "dud" to the person who called (just kidding).

• *Do you have a lively curiosity and no window in the lid of your bread machine?*

If you open the lid of the machine often, especially during the rising phase, you release the warm air the dough needs to rise properly.

• *Was the recipe high in fat or high in sugar?*
Limit the amount of each to ¼ cup (1-pound loaf) or ⅓ cup (1½-pound loaf).

• *Was your flour old and stale?*
Flour sold in the markets has a shelf life of 15 months but if it was stored improperly at home or allowed to get too hot or damp, it may have gone stale. Throw it out and buy a fresh bag.

• *Did you accidentally knock the machine or drop the lid during the rising phase?*
Sudden jolts can sometimes deflate a dough.

• *Did you use raw, unpasteurized honey?*
Heat it first (don't exceed 180°F).

• *Are you measuring your liquids by tablespoons rather than in a measuring cup?*
For the most accurate liquid measurement, use the measuring cup that came with your machine or a liquid measuring cup. Place it on a level surface and judge the amount at eye level.

❖❖❖

• *In the unlikely event you answered "no" to all the preceding questions, here are a few more bread-raising tips:*
Increase the amount of yeast and sugar slightly.
Replace a scant ¼ cup of the liquid with 1 egg for extra leavening.
Whole wheat breads can benefit from an extra kneading in most machines. After the first kneading cycle, stop the machine and restart it.
Try weighing your flour rather than measuring it. If you live in an area of the country that experiences extremes in weather conditions, weighing the flour will take the moisture content of the air and your flour into account. (See "Measurements" on page 47 for correct weights.)
Add lecithin (¼ teaspoon per cup of flour). It seems to work most effectively when combined with added gluten.
Keep in mind that a very tall loaf isn't always the ultimate objective. We've baked lid-thumpers that were all air and no body. Several of our favorite whole-grain breads are heavy, dense, and meant to be very thinly sliced.

Sunken Loaves: What Went Wrong

———————◆◆◆———————

• *Was the dough quite wet during the kneading cycle?*

Reduce the liquid in the recipe next time you bake that bread or add flour as it is mixing, 1 tablespoon at a time, until the dough forms a satiny-smooth ball.

• *Did you use a fast-rising or instant yeast?*

The dough may have overproofed. Use ½ teaspoon fast-rising or instant yeast per cup of flour.

• *Did you omit or greatly reduce the amount of salt?*

The salt helps prevent the dough from overproofing. For the bread to rise properly, you need to add some salt. If you want to reduce the amount of sodium, substitute Morton Lite Salt for table salt.

• *Was the machine knocked or the lid dropped near the end of the rising phase?*
A sudden jolt can deflate a loaf.

• *Is the bread machine in a drafty location?*
A cold draft can cause a bread to sink.

• *Do you live at an altitude above 7,000 feet?*
Refer to page 119 for suggestions on how to alter your recipes for high-altitude baking.

Loaves that Have Mushroom Tops or Overflow: How to Prevent Them

———————◆◆◆———————

• *Was the dough quite wet or did you add ingredients that increased the moisture content of the dough, such as fruits and vegetables?*

A too-wet dough can produce a variety of problems. In some cases, the bread will simply rise too high and overflow the pan; other times it will only threaten to overflow and produce a puffy, mushroomed top. An overly wet dough can also produce a bread that is very soft and spongy; when it's removed from the machine, the sides will collapse.

If you add extras that are moist, consider half their measure as liquid. Reduce the liquid in the recipe accordingly.

• *If the dough was very dry and crumbly while it was kneading, did you have to add more than 3 or 4 tablespoons of additional liquid to correct it?*

Next time, rather than adding so much more liquid, reduce the amount of flour instead.

- *Was the recipe too large for your machine?*

Recipes for 1-pound loaves consist of 2 cups of flour and approximately ⅞ cup of liquid. The 1½-pound recipe should have 3 cups of flour and about 1⅛ cups liquid. (In both cases, the amounts can be increased by approxmately ⅓ for whole-grain breads.) Using quantities much in excess of these can result in breads that will rise too high for the bread pan.

- *Did you omit or greatly reduce the amount of salt?*

Without salt, the yeast is uncontrolled and can produce a very tall loaf that will either collapse or overflow the pan.

- *Did the recipe call for a large amount of yeast?*

Reduce the yeast next time to 1½ to 2 teaspoons.

- *Was the recipe loaded with sweet ingredients?*

Try cutting back on the sugar in the future.

- *Did you use a fast-rising or instant yeast?*

This type of yeast can force a large loaf to rise too high, too quickly and exceed the bounds of the bread pan.

- *Was it a hot day?*

You'll find that your loaves will rise very enthusiastically when the weather is warm. To slow them down a bit, use colder liquids or choose a cooler time of day to bake.

- *Is this a favorite recipe that you're unwilling to alter, yet it consistently rises too high?*

Try baking it on the Rapid Bake cycle.

- *Did you go nuts with all those dough enhancers?*

If you threw in the works—gluten, lecithin, vinegar, ascorbic acid— were you all that surprised when it overflowed?

❖❖❖

A FEW EXTRA TIPS:

Just as it's a good habit to check the dough when it first begins mixing (ensuring that the mixing blade has been installed), it's also wise when you're home to peek at the bread near the end of the rising phase. If it is on the verge of overflowing the bread pan, you can prevent disaster by merely pricking the dough with a toothpick a few times to deflate it. It may not bake up picture perfect, but you'll save yourself a mammoth cleanup job. (We speak from experience.)

If it's a new recipe, try to be home the first time you make it to check on its progress occasionally.

An Assortment of Common Problems: Their Causes and Cures
◆◆◆

RAW, DOUGHY SPOTS IN THE CENTER OR TOP OF THE LOAF

• Too much heat escaped from the machine as the bread was baking.

• The recipe was too large for your machine.

• Too many rich or heavy ingredients and too short a Regular Bake cycle to bake the bread properly.

• If your bread machine has a glass dome, cover it with foil during the baking cycle. (Take care not to let the foil hang down and cover the air vents.)

• Use a smaller-size recipe next time.

• If your Regular Bake cycle is a Rapid Bake (3 hours or less), you may need to reduce the fat and/or added ingredients in certain recipes, such as raisin breads and holiday breads. They take too long to rise in Rapid-Bake machines unless lightened up.

A LARGE CRACK AROUND OR ON TOP OF THE LOAF

• The dough was too dry.

• The dough may have been underproofed; it didn't rise long enough before the Bake cycle began.

• Next time add 1 to 2 tablespoons more liquid.

• If you have a bread machine with the programmable feature, increase the rising time for that particular loaf.

IS IT A LOAF OF BREAD OR A DOORSTOP?— THE LOAF THAT NEVER EVEN MIXED; IT BAKED UP IN LAYERS AND WAS THREE INCHES TALL

• This one's easy . . . someone forgot to put the mixing blade in before adding all the ingredients.

• Another variation on that theme: You remembered the mixing blade but didn't insert it far enough down on the post.

• Variation #2: The blade was correctly installed but the bread pan itself was not well seated in the machine, so the mixing blade didn't engage properly.

BURNT CRUSTS

• Set the crust color to Light.

• Choose the Sweet Bread setting, if your machine has it.

• Reduce the amount of sugar.

• Remove the loaf from the machine five or ten minutes before the Bake cycle ends.

PALE LOAVES

• Increase the sugar.

• Add fresh or instant milk to the dough.

• Set the crust color darker.

A LARGE AIR BUBBLE UNDER THE CRUST OR IN THE CENTER OF THE LOAF

• The dough was not well mixed or didn't deflate properly during the "punch down" between risings.

• It's normally a rare occurrence; if it continues to happen in a particular loaf, try adding 1 or 2 tablespoons more liquid next time.

CRUST TOO TOUGH AND CHEWY

• Increase the fat in the recipe.

• Add more milk, less water.

• Brush the crust lightly with melted butter when you remove it from the pan.

• As soon as the bread cools, place it in a plastic bag. Don't allow it to sit out for hours.

• If your machine has a Cool Down cycle, leave the bread in the machine until the cooling cycle ends, rather than removing it immediately after the baking ends.

THE CRUST WAS TOO SOFT; YOU PREFER IT CRISP

• Reduce or eliminate the fat in your bread.

• Substitute water for milk in the recipe.

• Use the French Bread setting if your machine has it.

• As soon as the bread finishes baking, remove it from the bread pan.

• Do not place the bread in a plastic bag as soon as it cools.

THE CRUST WAS TOO CRISP; YOU PREFER IT SOFT

- Increase the fat in your bread.
- Use milk instead of water in the recipe.
- Do not use the French Bread setting.
- Allow the bread to cool in the machine, if it has a Cool Down cycle.
- When the bread cools completely, place it in a sealed plastic bag.

COARSE, HOLEY-TEXTURED BREADS

- The dough was too wet or contained too many wet ingredients.
- The salt was omitted.
- You substituted applesauce (or other puréed fruits) for the butter in the recipe but didn't reduce the liquid by an equal measure.
- Decrease the liquids.
- When adding "wet" ingredients such as fruits and vegetables, consider half their measure as liquid and adjust the other liquids in the recipe accordingly.

BLISTERS ON THE TOP OF THE LOAF

- The dough did not have a long enough rising time.
- If you have a machine with a programmable mode or a Whole Wheat cycle, use it to increase the rising time for that particular loaf.

STRONG YEASTY FLAVOR

- Reduce the amount of yeast next time.

SOFT-SIDED LOAVES THAT COLLAPSED ON ONE OR ALL SIDES

- The recipe had too much liquid.
- "Wet" ingredients were added to the dough and not taken into account.
- The bread was left in the pan after it finished baking and became very soggy.
- Reduce the liquid amount next time or add flour 1 tablespoon at a time during the kneading cycle.
- Remove the bread from the machine as soon as it is finished baking.

DRY BREAD

- Eggs cause breads to be drier than usual.

• Dry grains such as oatmeal were added, which soaked up moisture from the bread dough.

• Breads low in fat and/or sugar dry out rapidly.

• The bread was left out too long to cool and dried out.

• The bread was stored in the refrigerator.

• Add extra oil or fat to counteract eggs' drying effect.

• When adding dry grains to breads, either soak them first or increase the liquid in the recipe.

• Increase fat and/or sugar in the recipe.

• Replace granulated sugar with honey. Replace fat with an equal amount of applesauce.

• Ingredients such as fat, honey, fruits, and oatmeal help bread retain its moisture longer.

• Once bread has cooled, place it in a plastic bag.

• Breads stored in the refrigerator will dry out and turn stale several times faster than bread stored at room temperature.

COARSE, CRUMBLY TEXTURE

• The bread was too dry.

• It did not contain enough gluten.

• There may have been too many added cereals, grains, meals, and/or non-gluten flours.

• The salt was omitted.

• Dry, uncooked whole grains were added, which robbed the dough of its moisture.

• Reduce the amount of extra ingredients such as wheat bran, wheat germ, cornmeal, etc.

• Increase the liquid if the dough appears dry during kneading.

• When adding dry grains such as oats, multigrain cereal, or cornmeal, soak them first or increase the liquid in the recipe.

FUNKY, GNARLY SHAPED LOAVES

• This is a catchall category for any loaf that looks so weird, you're afraid to slice it open, much less offer samples to anyone you love.

• Sorry, you're on your own on this one!

• (If it's any consolation, even the "pros" goof up big time on occasion.

You haven't lived until you've almost burnt down a store at a book signing because you forgot to add the liquid to that herb bread you intended to bake. Nothing like a little smoke and the foul smell of burnt flour to entice customers to buy your cookbook.)

Refrigerating/Freezing Bread Dough
❖❖❖

REFRIGERATING DOUGH

• When the machine beeps, remove the dough from the pan and place it in a lightly oiled bowl with a tight-fitting lid or a large, oiled, plastic bag.

• You can store dough in the refrigerator for up to five days. Check it daily. It will rise very slowly and need punching down every day or so.

• When ready to use, remove the dough from the refrigerator 1½ to 2 hours before you plan to use it; this will bring it fully up to room temperature. (The time will vary according to the warmth of the room.) When the dough is room temperature, shape as desired, then place in a warm location to rise until doubled in size. Bake according to recipe directions.

• You can also remove the dough from the machine and shape it into dinner rolls, a loaf of bread, or a coffee cake. Cover and place the shaped dough in the coldest spot in the refrigerator. If made in the morning, you can bake it for dinner. Made at night, it will be ready for breakfast the next morning. Remove it from the refrigerator, let it come to room temperature, place in a warm location to rise until doubled in size, if necessary, then bake.

FREEZING DOUGH

• Remove the dough from the bread pan, shape as desired, wrap it up well, and freeze.

• Dough can be frozen for up to one month.

• When you're ready to use the dough, remove it from the freezer the night before and allow it to thaw in the refrigerator overnight.

• If you want to defrost the dough at room temperature, allow 3 to 4 hours. Small rolls may take only 2 hours. If the dough is shaped into a loaf, it may take up to 6 hours, depending on the warmth of the room.

• Once thawed, place the dough in a warm location to rise. You'll find that the dough will take quite a bit longer to rise than usual. Bake as directed.

❖

Here are just a few of the reasons to consider making a dough and then refrigerating or freezing it for later use:

• You can prepare a dough at your convenience and then bake it up fresh for a special meal. (We often do this with fat-free French bread dough because it goes stale so quickly if baked early in the day.)

• If the dough is prepared but something comes up, all is not lost. Just pop it into the refrigerator.

• It enables you to prepare dough in advance to take with you when you go camping for the weekend.

• You can prepare several batches of a dough in advance then bake them up all on the same day for a party or as gifts.

• You can duplicate a recipe that calls for double or triple the amount of ingredients your machine can handle by making it in batches, then combining them and baking the loaf in the oven.

• Prepare a pizza dough in the morning or the night before. When you come home from work, you can throw together a fabulous homemade pizza in less time than it takes to have one delivered!

• Freeze shaped dinner rolls on a cookie sheet (once frozen transfer to a plastic bag) and you can bake up just the quantity you desire for dinner and not the entire batch.

• You can prepare cinnamon rolls the night before and place them in the refrigerator to rise slowly. The next morning bring them to room temperature and bake them for breakfast. No need to get up at 4 A.M.!

• Prepare an apple strudel in the morning, let it slowly rise in the refrigerator all day, and bake it up as you sit down for dinner that night. It's a wonderful dessert after a light meal.

• Prepare the dough for hamburger buns and bake them up as needed. If you don't use all of the dough within five days, you can freeze it in single portions or go ahead and bake up the remaining buns and freeze them in heavy plastic bags to have on hand.

• When your grandchildren come to visit for several days, have dough on hand so you can make teddy bears or pita bread with them when there's a lull in the activities.

Storing Bread

◆◆◆

- To retain the crisp crust of French and sourdough breads, do not store them in plastic bags. Until sliced, you can leave them out as is. Once cut, place them in a large paper bag.

- When you remove the bread from the bread pan, place it on a rack to cool for at least one hour.

- Once fully cooled, place the loaf in a plastic bag, plastic container, or bread box. (Storage in plastic bags or containers will soften and change the bread's texture. You may prefer to store all your breads in paper; however, they will dry out and stale sooner than those stored in plastic.)

- If the bread is for immediate use, place it in a bag and leave it out at room temperature. Most breads will remain fresh for two to three days.

- To "freshen" and warm a several-day-old loaf for dinner, wrap it well in foil, heat at 300°F for 15 minutes until heated through.

- Breads made with honey, fruits, and fats will stay moist longer.

- Egg breads will dry out faster than usual. Adding extra oil to the bread will help counteract that.

- Do not store breads in the refrigerator. They will dry out and stale several times faster than when stored at room temperature.

- For longer storage, wrap the loaf well and place it in the freezer. It will keep up to three months there. To serve it warm at a meal, wrap the loaf in foil, place it in a 400°F oven for 10 minutes or so until heated through.

- Freezing destroys vitamin E.

- Though breads will not dry out as quickly if left whole when frozen, we prefer to slice the loaf once it cools and then place in plastic bags for freezing. That way, you can remove the number of slices desired from the bag without having to defrost the entire loaf for one or two slices.

- Thaw each slice in the microwave for about 15 seconds on HIGH.

Cleaning Your Machine

◆◆◆

- We've heard of people cleaning the inside of their bread machine with everything from a portable hand vacuum to the tiny vacuums used to clean computer keyboards. Lois has even used an eyebrow brush and an old toothbrush. Hey, whatever works! A few times around with a damp dishcloth or paper towel does the job, too. What you shouldn't do is turn your machine upside down and vigorously shake it.

• If your machine has a sensor in the bottom that activates a Preheating cycle, keep it clean and free of lint.

• As soon as you remove the bread from the pan, fill the pan with warm, soapy water. Let it sit for at least 10 minutes. That will enable you to remove the mixing blade without a great deal of trouble. If you allow the dough to dry out inside the blade, it will be a struggle trying to remove it.

• If the blade is difficult to remove, even after soaking, hold it with one hand and, with the other, hold the knob opposite it on the bottom of the pan. There should be a little give; move the blade back and forth until you can work it loose.

• It's easier to remove the bread dough from the mixing shaft in the Welbilt/DAK machines if you do so while it is still warm and soft. Use a damp dishcloth. If the dough is allowed to cool and harden, you will have to resoften it by wrapping a damp dishcloth around the shaft for several minutes to facilitate cleaning.

• The most effective way to clean the inside of the mixing blade is with the small end of a baby-bottle brush. It fits perfectly inside the hole.

• Wash the inside of the pan well with soapy water and a soft cloth or sponge. Do not use anything abrasive that will destroy the nonstick coating.

• Rinse the pan and mixing blade thoroughly. Any soap residue can interfere with the next bread you bake, causing a small loaf.

• Once they are clean, place all the little bits and pieces (such as the mixing blade, the dough pin, and the rubber seal) inside the pan so they won't disappear and cause a family crisis.

Our Favorite Accessories: The Little Extras that Add to the Fun of Baking Homemade Bread

If you've read the entire book up to this point, you deserve a break. It's time to go shopping! We thought we'd lighten it up a bit here and share the contents of our baking cabinets and gadget drawers. Over the years, the two of us have collected hundreds of "can't-live-without" kitchen tools and many of them are seeing new life as useful bread-baking accessories. Maybe one or two will strike your fancy, also. Here are some of our favorites:

• At the top of our list is a recent purchase that has made our lives so much easier. No more shortening under the fingernails or messy cookie sheets to clean. This new wonder is Von Snedaker's "Magic Baking Sheet," which we purchased at a local kitchen specialty store. It's a 17- by 14-inch sheet of pliable material that comes rolled up in a tube. You can cut it to fit your favorite cookie sheet, cake pans, or baking dishes. It makes every pan you use it in nonstick; no more greasing or flouring! You can use the magic baking sheet over and over again and it takes only a soapy sponging to clean it. Truly, it's one of those items that, once you use it, you wonder how you ever did without it.

• Favorite gadget #2 is a dough scraper. It just a piece of metal with a wooden handle across the top. When you're shaping dough, it's great for scraping the dough off the counter and also for cutting it into smaller pieces for rolls, bread sticks, etc. Haven't you seen TV spots where they show great pastry chefs using a dough scraper to manipulate the dough? Honest, that's what you'll feel like, too, when you work with one—a world-renowned bread chef! You'll be buying one of those fancy white hats, next.

• Our most often-used tool is a good serrated bread knife. If you have trouble cutting even slices, consider an electric knife, a fiddlebow knife (see Sources, page 189), or a small, portable food slicer. If you have a large Welbilt or DAK machine and want to cut perfect, round slices, DAK Industries sells a bread holder that will enable you to cut uniform ½-inch thick, round slices. (See page 192.)

• We both have citrus trees and like to add citrus peels to many of our breads. For that reason, Linda gets a great deal of use out of a zester. It's a

funny-looking little tool, a handle with a flat piece of metal at one end with several tiny holes across the top of the metal piece. It does a good job of removing just the flavorful outer peel and not the bitter white pith underneath. Lois's zester is more unique; she uses a Stanley Sureform shaver/woodworking tool. It's similar to a grater, has a wooden handle, and comes with extra blades.

• A pastry brush is invaluable when it comes to brushing melted butter on all those yummy cinnamon-roll doughs or oiling pizza pans.

• If you keep a kosher kitchen, order a second bread pan for your machine.

• Keep a roll of plain dental floss handy. When it comes time to slice those cinnamon rolls, instead of crushing them with a knife, place a long strand of dental floss underneath the roll, bring the ends up, cross them, and pull in opposite directions until you cut through the roll.

• At our local warehouse discount club, we discovered the large, rimmed, heavy baking sheets professional bakers use. They're a little larger than a jelly roll pan and work beautifully for all types of breads, rolls, and coffee cakes. Restaurant supply houses also carry them.

• We find it helpful to store things such as honey, molasses, and liquid lecithin in plastic squeeze bottles. (Make sure they were intended for food use.) They should be microwaveable, too. Linda has a row of little plastic honey bear squeeze bottles that greet her every time she opens her bread cupboard.

• Linda pulled her dehydrator out of storage, dusted it off, and put it to use again drying fruits, tomatoes, and fresh herbs for breads. The two appliances make a great duo.

• Another fun appliance that seems to go hand-in-hand with a bread machine is an electric snackmaker. You can turn a few slices of bread into all kinds of hot sandwiches and tidbits. Butter the outside of the bread slices, fill with anything from pizza ingredients to apple pie filling, close it up to bake, and in just a few minutes it's done! It's a great way to use up those last slices in each loaf. And for those of you with the round loaves of bread, DAK Industries has created a sandwichmaker for the Welbilt/DAK machine breads (see page 192).

• The least expensive item on the list: a $1 large aluminum salt shaker with a handle. (It's about 4 inches tall and 2½ inches in diameter.) Fill it with flour and use it for dusting your countertop when you roll out dough. It is also useful for giving country French breads a dusting of flour on top prior to baking.

• If you love crisp French bread, there are side-by-side French baguette pans made of a perforated metal (some are shiny, some are black) that yield the crispest crust possible next to a French bakery.

• We use a similar perforated pan for baking pizzas. It's 14 inches in diameter and produces a wonderful crisp pizza crust . . . no more soft or soggy bottoms.

• Another option for producing crisp French breads and pizza crusts is to bake them on a baking stone. Most gourmet cooking stores carry them.

• If your machine didn't include a measuring spoon, a set that includes a ½ tablespoon measure comes in very handy.

• A good pizza wheel to cut pizzas is a must if you bake your own quite often. Linda has an el-cheapo model that wobbles so much we should attach training wheels to it.

• You'll notice in our French Bread recipe (page 158) that we suggest letting the dough rise in a cloth-lined, round wicker basket for the most authentic loaf. The basket we used was 7 inches across the bottom, 3½ inches high, and 10 inches across the top. It worked beautifully.

• If you like to check the bread dough often as it kneads and during rising, a timer on a necklace will help you remember to do so when you're busy with other projects.

• Lois has a heavy ball-bearing rolling pin that she covers with a rolling pin cloth. Linda is eyeing it with envy. We've used it many times in our bread machine classes and it works like a charm.

• We've seen crumb boxes in several catalogs. They are the size of a small cutting board with wooden slats across the top. When you slice your bread on it, all the crumbs drop down into the box. There's no mess and they're attractive enough to use as a serving tray on your dining-room table.

• Good French bread is always a hit and we bake a lot of it. A plant mister stored above the oven comes in handy for spraying the bread with water as it bakes, to produce that crispy crust.

• We don't own one yet but we both have our eye on it: a good, large, wooden cutting board that hooks over the edge of the counter. They have one in the cooking school where we teach and it's a joy to work on.

• Linda's sister, Debbie, surprised her one Christmas with personalized paper bags that read "Baked especially for you in the oven of . . . [your name]" A large loaf of bread is pictured, also. They are *perfect* for all those gift breads. Miles Kimball still carries them (see page 192). Buy several sets; they go fast!

• King Arthur (see page 190) has various sizes of plastic storage bags for breads, including the hard-to-find bags for the large Panasonic loaves.

• Along the same lines, Lois also uses a product called Freeze-Tite. It's a very strong, heavy-duty plastic wrap that works well to keep breads fresh.

• This doesn't really fall into the category of accessories but its a great tip from Linda Caldwell, a very helpful friend to so many of us on our computer bulletin board. If your favorite cookbook is falling apart at the binding, check with your local Kinko's or any other business print shop. They can spiral-bind books for you at a reasonable cost.

✦✦✦ 6 ✦✦✦

Recipes

Recipes

The first eight recipes—San Diego Sunshine, Herb Bread, Jim's Cinnamon Rolls, DeDe's Buttermilk Bread, Anne and Bill's Apple Oatmeal Bread with Raisins, Sweet Lelani Bread, Whole Wheat Hamburger and Hot Dog Buns, and Jalapeño Cheese Bread—were originally published in our first book, *Bread Machine Magic*, and are back for an encore performance. We receive compliments on many of the breads in book number one but these eight seem to stand out. So if you're looking to start out with tried-and-true crowd pleasers, begin at the beginning.

We tested our recipes on eight different machines: several Panasonics; the Hitachi B101; the Zojirushi S-15; the Zojirushi N-15; the Welbilt ABM 100; and the Welbilt ABM 300/350. In order to create "generic" recipes to suit all machines, we had to make minor adjustments in some recipes, which we have noted. We also want to remind owners of the older 1½-pound Panasonic SD-BT6P that you will need to double the yeast amount in most recipes.

Each recipe can be baked on the standard Bake cycle; however, in the boxes at the end of each recipe we have also noted alternative baking cycles you might prefer to use, if your machine has them.

We have included a nutritional analysis at the end of each recipe to be used as a general guideline. The information was calculated on an average 1½-pound loaf containing fourteen ½-inch slices of bread.

We encourage you to experiment with these recipes and make them your own. We were rather restricted by trying to make every recipe work in every machine. You will have more freedom to add a dash of this and that to suit your taste buds and your particular machine. For instance, the basic white bread recipe for the Panasonic/National BT65 machine lists 6 tablespoons more flour and 2 tablespoons more liquid as their standard recipe. You may be more pleased with your Panasonic loaves if you add those amounts to our recipes.

So what are you waiting for? It's time to have some fun!

❖❖❖

SAN DIEGO SUNSHINE
◆◆◆

Just like our hometown, this bread will delight your senses! It's a sweet whole wheat loaf with a delicate hint of orange. Pack up a picnic basket with a thermos of hot coffee or tea, a loaf of this bread, and some honey butter. Locate a city park or a sunny terrace and you'll have the makings for a romantic, leisurely breakfast.

1½-POUND LOAF	1-POUND LOAF
1 cup water (for Welbilt/DAK and Zojirushi machines, add 2 tablespoons more water)	¾ cup water (for Welbilt machine, add 1 tablespoon more water)
2 tablespoons honey	1 tablespoon honey
2 cups bread flour	1⅓ cups bread flour
1 cup whole wheat flour	⅔ cup whole wheat flour
1 teaspoon salt	1 teaspoon salt
2 tablespoons butter or margarine	1½ tablespoons butter of margarine
2 tablespoons brown sugar	1 tablespoon brown sugar
Grated rind of 1½ oranges	Grated rind of 1 orange
2 teaspoons Red Star brand active dry yeast	1½ teaspoons Red Star brand active dry yeast

1. Place all ingredients in bread pan, select Light Crust setting, and press Start.

2. After the baking cycle ends, remove bread from pan, place on cake rack, and allow to cool 1 hour before slicing.

CRUST: LIGHT
OPTIONAL BAKE CYCLES:
   SWEET BREAD
   DELAYED TIMER

NUTRITIONAL INFORMATION
PER SLICE

Calories	127
Fat	1.9 grams
Carbohydrate	24.6 grams
Protein	3.2 grams
Fiber	1.7 grams
Sodium	169 milligrams
Cholesterol	4.4 milligrams

DEDE'S BUTTERMILK BREAD
✦✦✦

This bread is by far the most popular bread from our first book, *Bread Machine Magic.* Two slices from this moist, rich, and tender loaf will make any sandwich exceptional.

1½-POUND LOAF

1⅛ cups buttermilk (for Welbilt/DAK and Zojirushi machines, add 2 tablespoons more buttermilk)
3 tablespoons honey
3 cups bread flour
1½ teaspoons salt
1 tablespoon butter or margarine
2 teaspoons Red Star brand active dry yeast

1-POUND LOAF

⅞ cups buttermilk (for Welbilt machine, add 1 tablespoon more buttermilk)
2 tablespoons honey
2 cups bread flour
1 teaspoon salt
1 tablespoon butter or margarine
1½ teaspoons Red Star brand active dry yeast

1. Place all ingredients in bread pan, select Light Crust setting, and press Start.

2. After the baking cycle ends, remove bread from pan, place on cake rack, and allow to cool 1 hour before slicing.

CRUST: LIGHT
OPTIONAL BAKE CYCLES:
SWEET BREAD

NUTRITIONAL INFORMATION PER SLICE	
Calories	127
Fat	1.3 grams
Carbohydrate	25.1 grams
Protein	3.5 grams
Fiber	.8 gram
Sodium	257 milligrams
Cholesterol	2.9 milligrams

ANNE AND BILL'S
APPLE OATMEAL BREAD WITH RAISINS
✦✦✦

Oatmeal and applesauce combine to make this a lush, rich-tasting loaf. It's a good snack for children and great for breakfast toast.

1½-POUND LOAF	1-POUND LOAF
½ cups old-fashioned rolled oats	⅓ cup old-fashioned rolled oats
⅝ cup water (for Welbilt/DAK and Zojirushi machines, add 2 tablespoons more water)	½ cup water (for Welbilt machine, add 1 tablespoon more water)
½ cup unsweetened applesauce	⅓ cup unsweetened applesauce
2¾ cups bread flour	1¾ cups bread flour
1½ teaspoons salt	1 teaspoon salt
1½ tablespoons butter or margarine	1 tablespoon butter or margarine
2 tablespoons brown sugar	1 tablespoon brown sugar
1½ tablespoons nonfat dry milk powder	1 tablespoon nonfat dry milk powder
⅓ cup raisins	¼ cup raisins
1 teaspoon ground cinnamon	1 teaspoon ground cinnamon
2 teaspoons Red Star brand active dry yeast	1½ teaspoons Red Star brand active dry yeast

1. Place all ingredients in bread pan, select Light Crust setting, and press Start.

2. After the baking cycle ends, remove bread from pan, place on cake rack, and allow to cool 1 hour before slicing.

CRUST: LIGHT
OPTIONAL BAKE CYCLES:
  SWEET BREAD
  RAISIN/NUT
  RAPID BAKE
  DELAYED TIMER
	**NUTRITIONAL INFORMATION
	PER SLICE**
	Calories 114
	Fat .5 gram
	Carbohydrate 23.8 grams
	Protein 3.4 grams
	Fiber 1.3 grams
	Sodium 232 milligrams
	Cholesterol .1 milligram

HERB BREAD

✦✦✦

Plan to be around while this one bakes, because the aroma is absolutely out of this world! As for the taste, it's hard to limit yourself to just one slice of this zesty bread. We recommend it for croutons, also. (Note: When making the 1-pound loaf, use the Rapid Bake setting for a better-shaped bread.)

1½-POUND LOAF	1-POUND LOAF
3 tablespoons butter or margarine	2 tablespoons butter or margarine
½ cup chopped onion	⅓ cup chopped onion
1 cup milk (for Welbilt/DAK and Zojirushi machines, add 2 tablespoons more milk)	¾ cup milk (for Welbilt machine, add 1 tablespoon more milk)
3 cups bread flour	2 cups bread flour
1½ teaspoons salt	1 teaspoon salt
1½ tablespoons sugar	1 tablespoon sugar
½ teaspoon dried dill	½ teaspoon dried dill
½ teaspoon dried basil	½ teaspoon dried basil
½ teaspoon dried rosemary	½ teaspoon dried rosemary
2 teaspoons Red Star brand active dry yeast	1½ teaspoons Red Star brand active dry yeast

1. In a small skillet, melt butter over low heat. Add onion and sauté 8 to 10 minutes until onion is soft but not brown. Remove from heat; allow mixture to cool for 10 minutes before adding it to the bread pan.

FOR 1½-POUND LOAF

Place all ingredients (including onion mixture) in bread pan, select Light Crust setting, and press Start.

After the baking cycle ends, remove bread from pan, place on cake rack, and allow to cool 1 hour before slicing.

```
CRUST: LIGHT
```

FOR 1-POUND LOAF

Place all ingredients (including onion mixture) in bread pan, select Rapid Bake setting, and press Start.

After the baking cycle ends, remove bread from pan, place on cake rack, and allow to cool 1 hour before slicing.

```
CRUST: MEDIUM
```

NUTRITIONAL INFORMATION PER SLICE	
Calories	138
Fat	3.3 grams
Carbohydrate	23.2 grams
Protein	3.5 grams
Fiber	.9 gram
Sodium	259 milligrams
Cholesterol	9 milligrams

JIM'S CINNAMON ROLLS
✦✦✦

Nothing can top the aroma and warm, sweet stickiness of cinnamon rolls, fresh from the oven. What you'll also love about these luscious, light rolls is that the machine does half the work; they're no longer a major production. The first time Lois made these, her husband Jim emphatically declared them his favorite recipe of all—high praise from one who had been completely noncommittal about the breads until then!

1½-POUND	1-POUND
DOUGH	**DOUGH**
⅜ cup milk	¼ cup milk
⅜ cup water (for Welbilt/DAK and Zojirushi machines, add 2 tablespoons more water)	¼ cup water (for Welbilt machine, add 1 tablespoon more water)
1 egg	1 egg
3 cups all-purpose flour	2 cups all-purpose flour
1 teaspoon salt	1 teaspoon salt
4 tablespoons butter or margarine	3 tablespoons butter or margarine
⅓ cup sugar	¼ cup sugar
1½ teaspoons Red Star brand active dry yeast	1½ teaspoons Red Star brand active dry yeast
GLAZE	**GLAZE**
5 tablespoons melted butter or margarine	3 tablespoons melted butter or margarine
½ cup brown sugar	½ cup brown sugar
FILLING	**FILLING**
1 tablespoon melted butter or margarine	1 tablespoon melted butter or margarine
2 tablespoons granulated sugar	1 tablespoon granulated sugar
1 tablespoon ground cinnamon	1½ teaspoons ground cinnamon
2 tablespoons brown sugar	1 tablespoon brown sugar
½ cup raisins, optional	⅓ cup raisins, optional

1. Place dough ingredients in bread pan, select Dough setting, and press Start.

2. When dough has risen long enough, the machine will beep. Turn off bread machine, remove bread pan, and turn out dough onto a floured countertop or cutting board.

FOR 1½-POUND DOUGH

Pour the melted butter for the glaze into one 9 × 13 × 2 inch pan or two 8- or 9 inch round cake pans; sprinkle with brown sugar. With a rolling pin, roll dough into a 9 × 18 inch rectangle.

FOR 1-POUND DOUGH

Pour the melted butter for the glaze into one 9-inch round or square cake pan; sprinkle with brown sugar. With a rolling pin, roll dough into an 8 × 14-inch rectangle.

FOR THE FILLING

3. Brush the melted butter on the dough. In a small bowl, combine the granulated sugar, cinnamon, brown sugar, and raisins; sprinkle over dough. Starting with long edge, roll up dough; pinch seams to seal. With a knife, lightly mark roll into 1½-inch sections. Slide a 12-inch piece of dental floss or heavy thread underneath. By bringing the ends of the floss up and crisscrossing them at the top of each mark, you can cut through the roll by pulling the strings in opposite directions. Place rolls cut side up in prepared pan(s), flattening them slightly.* Cover and let rise in a warm oven 30 to 45 minutes until doubled. (Hint: To warm oven slightly, turn over on Warm setting for 1 minute, then turn it off, and place covered dough in oven to rise. Remove pan[s] from oven to preheat.)

4. Preheat oven to 350°F. Bake 25 to 30 minutes until golden brown. Remove from oven and immediately invert rolls onto a large platter or serving dish. Serve warm.

1½-pound dough yields 12 rolls
1-pound dough yields 9 rolls

BAKE CYCLE: DOUGH

NUTRITIONAL INFORMATION PER ROLL	
Calories	302
Fat	10.6 grams
Carbohydrate	48.1 grams
Protein	4.4 grams
Fiber	1.4 grams
Sodium	274 milligrams
Cholesterol	44.7 milligrams

*The rolls can be covered with foil at this point and refrigerated overnight or frozen for 1 month. Before baking, allow rolls to thaw completely and rise in a warm oven for at least 30 minutes.

WHOLE WHEAT HAMBURGER AND HOT DOG BUNS

◆◆◆

These are definitely five-star hamburger buns. You'll never go back to the store-bought version once you've tried these.

1½-POUND	1-POUND
1 cup water (for Welbilt/DAK and Zojirushi machines, add 2 tablespoons more water)	⅝ cup water (for Welbilt machine, add 1 tablespoon more water)
1 egg	1 egg
2 cups all-purpose flour	1⅓ cups all-purpose flour
1 cup whole wheat flour	⅔ cup whole wheat flour
¾ teaspoon salt	½ teaspoon salt
¼ cup shortening	3 tablespoons shortening
¼ cup sugar	3 tablespoons sugar
3 teaspoons Red Star brand active dry yeast	2 teaspoons Red Star brand active dry yeast

1. Place dough ingredients in bread pan, select Dough setting, and press Start.

2. When the dough has risen long enough, the machine will beep. Turn off bread machine, remove bread pan, and turn out dough onto a lightly floured countertop or cutting board. Gently roll and shape the dough into a 12-inch rope.

FOR 1½-POUND DOUGH

With a sharp knife, divide dough into 10 pieces for hamburger buns and 12 pieces for hot dog buns.

FOR 1-POUND DOUGH

With a sharp knife, divide dough into 7 pieces for hamburger buns or 8 pieces for hot dog buns.

3. Grease a baking sheet. Roll pieces of dough into balls and flatten for hamburger buns or shape into 6-inch rolls for hot dog buns. Place on prepared baking sheet. Cover and let rise in a warm oven 10 to 15 minutes until almost doubled. (Hint: To warm oven slightly, turn oven on Warm setting for 1 minute, then turn it off, and place covered dough in oven to rise. Remove sheet from oven to preheat.)

4. Preheat oven to 400°F. Bake 12 to 15 minutes until golden brown. Remove from oven and cool on racks. When ready to use, split buns in half horizontally. These will keep in a plastic bag in the freezer for 3 to 4 weeks.

1½-pound dough yields 10 hamburger or 12 hot dog buns
1-pound dough yields 7 hamburger or 8 hot dog buns

MENU SELECTION: DOUGH

NUTRITIONAL INFORMATION PER HAMBURGER BUN	
Calories	206
Fat	6.1 grams
Carbohydrate	32.9 grams
Protein	5.1 grams
Fiber	2.4 grams
Sodium	168 milligrams
Cholesterol	21.3 milligrams

NUTRITIONAL INFORMATION PER HOT DOG BUN	
Calories	171
Fat	5.1 grams
Carbohydrate	27.4 grams
Protein	4.3 grams
Fiber	2 grams
Sodium	140 milligrams
Cholesterol	17.7 milligrams

SWEET LELANI BREAD
✦✦✦

This Hawaiian-style bread is a spectacular addition to any luncheon buffet. It's moist, light, and elegant. Don't let the long list of ingredients prevent you from trying this bread. It's definitely one of the best in the book.

1½-POUND LOAF	1-POUND LOAF
½ cup canned pineapple chunks, cut up and well drained (reserve juice)	⅓ cup canned pineapple chunks, cut up and well drained (reserve juice)
¼ cup buttermilk (for Welbilt/DAK and Zojirushi machines, add 2 tablespoons more buttermilk)	3 tablespoons buttermilk (for Welbilt machine, add 1 tablespoon more buttermilk)
¼ cup reserved pineapple juice	2 tablespoons reserved pineapple juice
1 egg	1 egg
½ cup sliced very ripe banana	⅓ cup sliced very ripe banana
3 cups bread flour	2 cups bread flour
¼ cup whole wheat flour	3 tablespoons whole wheat flour
1 teaspoon salt	1 teaspoon salt
3 tablespoons butter or margarine	2 tablespoons butter or margarine
1½ tablespoons sugar	1 tablespoon sugar
½ cup shredded coconut	⅓ cup shredded coconut
⅓ cup chopped macadamia nuts	¼ cup chopped macadamia nuts
2 teaspoons Red Star brand active dry yeast	1½ teaspoons Red Star brand active dry yeast

1. Place all ingredients in bread pan, select Light Crust setting, and press Start.

2. After the baking cycle ends, remove bread from pan, place on cake rack, and allow to cool 1 hour before slicing.

CRUST: LIGHT
OPTIONAL BAKE CYCLES:
SWEET BREAD
RAISIN/NUT

NUTRITIONAL INFORMATION PER SLICE	
Calories	191
Fat	6.8 grams
Carbohydrate	28.7 grams
Protein	4.2 grams
Fiber	1.8 grams
Sodium	215 milligrams
Cholesterol	22 milligrams

JALAPEÑO CHEESE BREAD

✦✦✦

Wow—hot stuff! Serve this coarsely textured, very spicy bread at your next cocktail party and watch it disappear. It's great with a glass of wine or a cold beer, but its perfect partner is a frosty margarita!

1½-POUND LOAF	1-POUND LOAF
¾ cup sour cream	½ cup sour cream
⅛ cup water (for Welbilt/DAK and Zojirushi machines, add 2 tablespoons more water)	⅛ cup water (for Welbilt machine, add 1 tablespoon more water)
1 egg	1 egg
3 cups all-purpose flour	2 cups all-purpose flour
1½ teaspoons salt	1 teaspoon salt
2 tablespoons sugar	1½ tablespoons sugar
1 cup (4 ounces) grated sharp Cheddar cheese	¾ cup (3 ounces) grated sharp Cheddar cheese
3 tablespoons seeded and chopped fresh jalapeño pepper (about 4 peppers) or canned diced jalapeño peppers	2 tablespoons seeded and chopped fresh jalapeño pepper (about 3 peppers) or canned diced jalapeño peppers
2 teaspoons Red Star brand active dry yeast	1½ teaspoons Red Star brand active dry yeast

1. Place all ingredients in bread pan, select Light Crust setting, and press Start.

2. After the baking cycle ends, remove bread from pan, place on cake rack, and allow to cool 1 hour before slicing.

CRUST: LIGHT

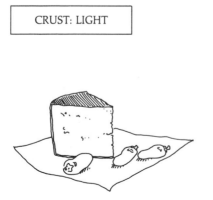

NUTRITIONAL INFORMATION PER SLICE	
Calories	169
Fat	5.9 grams
Carbohydrate	23 grams
Protein	5.7 grams
Fiber	.9 gram
Sodium	305 milligrams
Cholesterol	29.2 milligrams

JIM'S MAPLE WALNUT BREAD
◆◆◆

Jim Bodle of Clockville, New York, sent us this recipe. He loves just about anything that has maple syrup in it so once he purchased his bread machine, he decided to create a maple syrup bread. We're certainly glad he did! This bread was a huge hit when shared with friends.

1½-POUND LOAF	1-POUND LOAF
⅞ cup water (for Welbilt/DAK and Zojirushi machines, add 1 tablespoon more water)	⅝ cup water (for Welbilt machine, add 1 tablespoon more water)
½ cup maple syrup	¼ cup maple syrup
3 cups bread flour	2 cups bread flour
1 teaspoon salt	¾ teaspoon salt
1 tablespoon butter or margarine	2 teaspoons butter or margarine
1 tablespoon sugar	2 teaspoons sugar
2 tablespoons nonfat dry milk powder	1½ tablespoons nonfat dry milk powder
¼ cup walnuts, chopped	3 tablespoons walnuts, chopped
1½ teaspoons Red Star brand active dry yeast	2 teaspoons Red Star brand active dry yeast

1. Place all ingredients in bread pan, select Light Crust setting, and press Start.

2. After the baking cycle ends, remove bread from pan, place on cake rack, and allow to cool 1 hour before slicing.

CRUST: LIGHT
OPTIONAL BAKE CYCLES:
SWEET BREAD
RAISIN/NUT
RAPID BAKE
DELAYED TIMER

NUTRITIONAL INFORMATION PER SLICE	
Calories	153
Fat	2.4 grams
Carbohydrate	29.5 grams
Protein	3.4 grams
Fiber	.9 gram
Sodium	165 milligrams
Cholesterol	2.3 milligrams

LINDA'S LEMON BREAD
✦✦✦

This sweet/sour, moist bread has a bright fresh taste and smells marvelous even when it's kneading. Lemon curd can be found in either the jam/jelly section of your market or with the gourmet/imported foods. Some lazy afternoon, treat yourself to a cup of tea and a slice of this special bread.

1½-POUND LOAF

⅔ cup old-fashioned rolled oats
1⅛ cups milk (for Welbilt/DAK and Zojirushi machines, add 4 tablespoons more milk)
½ cup lemon curd
3 cups bread flour
1½ teaspoons salt
1½ tablespoons butter or margarine
2 teaspoons Red Star brand active dry yeast

1-POUND LOAF

½ cup old-fashioned rolled oats
⅞ cup milk (for Welbilt machine, add 1 tablespoon more milk)
⅓ cup lemon curd
2⅛ cups bread flour
1 teaspoon salt
1 tablespoon butter or margarine
1½ teaspoons Red Star brand active dry yeast

1. Place the ingredients in the bread pan, insert it into the machine, select a Light Crust setting and press Start.

2. After the baking cycle ends, remove bread from pan, place on cake rack, and allow to cool for 1 hour before slicing.

CRUST: LIGHT
OPTIONAL BAKE CYCLES:
  SWEET BREAD
  RAPID BAKE

NUTRITIONAL INFORMATION
PER SLICE

Calories	174
Fat	3.4 grams
Carbohydrate	31.9 grams
Protein	4.2 grams
Fiber	1.4 grams
Sodium	252 milligrams
Cholesterol	6 milligrams

BUTTERMILK HONEY BRAN BREAD

✦✦✦

This bakes up into a lovely, tall loaf flecked with bran and with a wholesome taste.

1½-POUND LOAF	1-POUND LOAF
½ cup miller's bran	⅓ cup miller's bran
1¼ cups buttermilk (for Welbilt/DAK and Zojirushi machines, add 1 tablespoon more buttermilk)	⅞ cup buttermilk (for Welbilt machine, add 1 tablespoon more buttermilk)
3 tablespoons honey	2 tablespoons honey
3 cups bread flour	2 cups bread flour
1½ teaspoons salt	¾ teaspoon salt
1½ tablespoons butter or margarine	1 tablespoon butter or margarine
1½ teaspoons Red Star brand active dry yeast	1½ teaspoons Red Star brand active dry yeast

1. Place all ingredients in bread pan, select Light Crust setting, and press Start.

2. After the baking cycle ends, remove bread from pan, place on cake rack, and allow to cool 1 hour before slicing.

CRUST: LIGHT
OPTIONAL BAKE CYCLE:
SWEET BREAD
RAPID BAKE

NUTRITIONAL INFORMATION PER SLICE	
Calories	136
Fat	1.8 grams
Carbohydrate	26.6 grams
Protein	3.9 grams
Fiber	1.4 grams
Sodium	263 milligrams
Cholesterol	4.1 milligrams

JANA'S SEED AND NUT BREAD

✦✦✦

We shared this glorious loaf with the staff of J.C.'s Kitchen Company in San Diego, people with very discriminating taste buds. To our delight, it earned a unanimous thumbs-up! So we thought it fitting to name it in honor of the store's owner, Jana Cason. Jana suggests serving it with a flavored cream-cheese spread. (Note: We had some problems with this loaf overflowing in the 1-pound machines occasionally. We recommend you keep an eye on it the first time you try it.)

1½-POUND LOAF	1-POUND LOAF
1⅛ cups water (for Welbilt/DAK and Zojirushi machines, add 1 tablespoon more water)	⅝ cup water (for Welbilt machine, no extra water is needed)
1 egg	1 egg
2 tablespoons oil	2 tablespoons oil
3 cups bread flour	2¼ cups bread flour
2 teaspoons salt	1½ teaspoons salt
¼ cup brown sugar	3 tablespoons brown sugar
1 cup chopped pecans, toasted*	½ cup chopped pecans, toasted*
¼ cup raw, unsalted sunflower seeds, toasted*	2 tablespoons raw, unsalted sunflower seeds, toasted*
¼ cup chopped walnuts, toasted*	2 tablespoons chopped walnuts, toasted*
1½ teaspoons Red Star brand active dry yeast	1½ teaspoons Red Star brand active dry yeast

1. Place all ingredients in bread pan, select Light Crust setting, and press Start.

2. After the baking cycle ends, remove bread from pan, place on cake rack, and allow to cool 1 hour before slicing.

CRUST: LIGHT
OPTIONAL BAKE CYCLES:
RAISIN/NUT
SWEET BREAD
RAPID BAKE

NUTRITIONAL INFORMATION PER SLICE	
Calories	221
Fat	10.9 grams
Carbohydrate	26.7 grams
Protein	4.9 grams
Fiber	1.7 grams
Sodium	312 milligrams
Cholesterol	15.2 milligrams

*To toast pecans, walnuts, and sunflower seeds, place them in a small pan and bake in a 350°F oven for 5 minutes.

SHAYNA'S VEGAN BURGERS

✦✦✦

These hearty "burgers" came in mighty handy when Linda's daughter Shayna needed something quick to pack for lunch. There are endless combinations of filling ingredients you can try.

1½-POUND

DOUGH

1 cup water (for Welbilt/DAK and Zojirushi machines, add 2 tablespoons more water)
1½ cups all-purpose flour
1½ cups whole wheat flour
1 teaspoon salt
2 tablespoons olive oil
3 tablespoons sugar
2 teaspoons Red Star brand active dry yeast

FILLING

2 cups freshly cooked or canned black beans, rinsed, drained
2 cups frozen corn kernels, thawed, drained
2 cups cooked brown rice
½ cup chopped green pepper (about ½ large pepper)
2 teaspoons ground cumin
1 teaspoon chili powder
1 teaspoon salt, optional
½ cup salsa or picante sauce

1-POUND

DOUGH

¾ cup water (for Welbilt machine, add 1 tablespoon more water)
1 cup all-purpose flour
1 cup whole wheat flour
¾ teaspoon salt
1½ tablespoons olive oil
2 tablespoons sugar
2 teaspoons Red Star brand active dry yeast

FILLING

1⅓ cups freshly cooked or canned black beans, rinsed, drained
1⅓ cups frozen corn kernels, thawed, drained
1⅓ cups cooked brown rice
⅓ cup chopped green pepper (about ½ small pepper)
1½ teaspoons ground cumin
¾ teaspoon chili powder
¾ teaspoon salt, optional
⅓ cup salsa or picante sauce

1. Place dough ingredients in bread pan, select Dough setting, and press Start.

2. Meanwhile, in a large bowl, combine filling ingredients. Set aside. Grease a large baking sheet.

3. When the dough has risen long enough, the machine will beep. Turn off bread machine, remove bread pan, and turn out dough onto a lightly floured countertop or cutting board. Gently roll or stretch dough into a 12-inch rope.

FOR 1½-POUND DOUGH

With a sharp knife, divide the dough into 12 pieces.

FOR 1-POUND DOUGH

With a sharp knife, divide the dough into 8 pieces.

4. With a rolling pin, roll each piece into a 6-inch circle. Place ½ cup filling mixture in the center of each circle. Pull the edges up to meet in the center and pinch dough together well to seal. Place on prepared baking sheet, sealed side down. Cover and let rise in a warm oven 15 minutes. (Hint: To warm oven slightly, turn oven on Warm setting for 1 minute, then turn it off, and place covered dough in oven to rise. Remove baking sheet from oven to preheat.)

5. Preheat oven to 400°F. Bake for 15 to 20 minutes until brown. Remove from oven. Serve warm or cold with additional salsa and/or guacamole. These freeze well in a plastic bag for up to 3 months. To reheat, place in a 325°F oven for 30 minutes or microwave on HIGH power for 1½ to 2 minutes.

FILLING VARIATIONS:

Vegetables: Cooked carrots, broccoli, celery, cabbage, onions, peas, spinach, turnips, potatoes, etc.

Grains: Cooked couscous, tabouleh, wild rice, white rice, bulgur, kasha, etc.

Legumes: Cooked or canned kidney beans, garbanzo beans, pinto beans, lima beans, lentils, split peas, etc.

Seasonings: Curry powder, lemon pepper, chili powder, freshly ground pepper, various herbs, barbecue sauce, spaghetti sauce, humus, tahini, etc.

1½-pound dough yields 12 burgers
1-pound dough yields 8 burgers

BAKE CYCLE: DOUGH

NUTRITIONAL INFORMATION PER BURGER	
Calories	216
Fat	3.1 grams
Carbohydrates	41.3 grams
Protein	7.6 grams
Fiber	6.6 grams
Sodium	504 milligrams
Cholesterol	0 milligrams

FRENCH BREAD EXTRAORDINAIRE!
❖❖❖

This method, though time-consuming, produces an exceptional loaf of French bread much like the ones baked in the boulangeries of Paris. The extra risings fully develop the bread's flavor. (Do not use the Crisp Dough cycle on the 1½-pound Panasonic/National.) The finished loaf will have a crisp crust and very moist, chewy interior. *Bon appétit!*

1½-POUND

1¼ cups water (for Welbilt/DAK and Zojirushi machines, add 2 tablespoons more water)
3½ cups unbleached white flour
1½ teaspoons salt
2 teaspoons Red Star brand active dry yeast

1-POUND

⅞ cup water (for Welbilt machine, add 1 tablespoon more water)
2⅓ cups unbleached white flour
1 teaspoon salt
2 teaspoons Red Star brand active dry yeast

1. Place dough ingredients in bread pan, select Dough setting, and press Start.

2. When the dough cycle ends, the machine will beep. Set a timer and allow the dough to rise 1 more hour. Open the machine, punch down the dough, set the timer again and let dough rise another hour in the machine. Turn off bread machine, remove bread pan, and turn out dough onto a lightly floured countertop or cutting board. Form into a smooth, round ball then flatten it with your hands.

3. Place a clean kitchen towel (not terry cloth) in a round wicker basket that's at least twice the size of the dough. Dust the towel liberally with flour. Place the round dough in the center of the basket. Place basket in a warm place and let dough rise, uncovered, about 45 minutes until double in size.

4. Gently turn dough out of basket upside down onto a greased baking sheet. With a very sharp knife held almost parallel to the loaf, carefully slash the top of the dough at sharp angles in a # pattern.

5. Preheat oven to 450°F. Place a small pan on the floor or bottom shelf of the oven and carefully add at least 1 cup boiling water to the pan. Place dough in oven and bake for 20 minutes. Remove from oven and place on cake rack to cool 1 hour before slicing. To preserve the crisp crust, do not store in plastic wrap or bag. Bread can be loosely covered or left out for up to two days before it dries out completely.

BAKE CYCLE: DOUGH

NUTRITIONAL INFORMATION PER SLICE	
Calories	115
Fat	.3 gram
Carbohydrate	23.9 grams
Protein	3.4 grams
Fiber	.9 gram
Sodium	230 milligrams
Cholesterol	0 milligrams

QUAKER MULTIGRAIN BREAD
❖❖❖

Quaker now makes a multigrain cereal that looks much like their famous oats but it's a combination of rye, barley, oats, and wheat flakes. We think this new cereal is a perfect ingredient to add to your breads. (Note: This is a small loaf. If you choose to add gluten, increase the buttermilk by 1 or 2 tablespoons as well.)

1½-POUND LOAF	1-POUND LOAF
1 cup Quaker Multigrain cereal	⅔ cup Quaker Multigrain cereal
1¼ cups buttermilk (for Welbilt/DAK and Zojirushi machines, add 3 tablespoons more buttermilk)	¾ cup buttermilk (for Welbilt machine, add 1 tablespoon more buttermilk)
3 tablespoons molasses	2 tablespoons molasses
2 cups bread flour	1⅓ cups bread flour
½ cup whole wheat flour	⅓ cup whole wheat flour
1½ teaspoons salt	1 teaspoon salt
1½ tablespoons butter or margarine	1 tablespoon butter or margarine
3½ tablespoons gluten, optional	2 tablespoons gluten, optional
2 teaspoons Red Star brand active dry yeast	2 teaspoons Red Star brand active dry yeast

1. Place all ingredients in bread pan, select Light Crust setting, and press Start.

2. After the baking cycle ends, remove bread from pan, place on cake rack, and allow to cool 1 hour before slicing.

CRUST: LIGHT
OPTIONAL BAKE CYCLES:
SWEET BREAD
RAPID BAKE
WHOLE WHEAT

NUTRITIONAL INFORMATION PER SLICE	
Calories	139
Fat	1.9 grams
Carbohydrates	26 grams
Protein	5.2 grams
Fiber	1.4 grams
Sodium	264 milligrams
Cholesterol	4.1 milligrams

WHOLE WHEAT
CINNAMON RAISIN BREAD
❖❖❖

This dark, rich bread is scrumptious! Try it for breakfast, either plain or toasted. (Note: If you have a machine with a regular baking cycle of under 3 hours, you may need to reduce the amount of butter by half if you find it didn't rise well the first time.)

1½-POUND LOAF	1-POUND LOAF
⅞ cup buttermilk (for Welbilt/DAK machines, add 2 tablespoons more buttermilk; For the Zojirushi, add 3 tablespoons more buttermilk)	⅝ cup buttermilk (for Welbilt machine, add 1 tablespoon more buttermilk)
1 egg	1 egg
1½ cups whole wheat flour	1 cup whole wheat flour
1½ cups bread flour	1¼ cups bread flour
1 teaspoon salt	¾ teaspoon salt
⅓ cup butter or margarine	¼ cup butter or margarine
3 tablespoons brown sugar	2 tablespoons brown sugar
⅔ cup raisins	½ cup raisins
1 teaspoon cinnamon	¾ teaspoon cinnamon
2 teaspoons Red Star brand active dry yeast	1½ teaspoons Red Star brand active dry yeast

1. Place all ingredients in bread pan, select Light Crust setting, and press Start.

2. After the baking cycle ends, remove bread from pan, place on cake rack, and allow to cool 1 hour before slicing.

CRUST: LIGHT
OPTIONAL BAKE CYCLES:
SWEET BREAD
RAISIN/NUT
WHOLE WHEAT

NUTRITIONAL INFORMATION PER SLICE	
Calories	175
Fat	5.2 grams
Carbohydrate	28.7 grams
Protein	4.5 grams
Fiber	2.5 grams
Sodium	212 milligrams
Cholesterol	27.5 milligrams

LOIS'S COUNTRY CRUNCH BREAD

<hr>

This chewy loaf is Lois's favorite. When she tried it for the first time, she exclaimed, "Now this is what bread should taste like!" (Note: In the Zojirushi, we had better results when we baked it on the Regular cycle rather than the French Bread cycle.)

1½-POUND LOAF	1-POUND LOAF
1⅛ cups water (for Welbilt/DAK and Zojirushi machines, add 1 tablespoon more water)	⅞ cup water (for Welbilt machine, add 1 tablespoon more water)
3 cups bread flour	2 cups bread flour
1½ teaspoons salt	1 teaspoon salt
½ tablespoon butter or margarine	1 teaspoon butter or margarine
1½ teaspoons sugar	1 teaspoon sugar
2 teaspoons Red Star brand active dry yeast	1½ teaspoons Red Star brand active dry yeast

1. Place all ingredients in bread pan and press Start.

2. After the baking cycle ends, remove bread from pan, place on cake rack, and allow to cool 1 hour before slicing.

CRUST: MEDIUM
OPTIONAL BAKE CYCLES:
    FRENCH BREAD
    RAPID BAKE
    DELAYED TIMER

VARIATION:

1. Place dough ingredients in bread pan, select Dough setting, and press Start.

2. When the dough has risen long enough, the machine will beep. Turn off bread machine, remove bread pan, and turn out dough onto a lightly floured countertop or cutting board. Shape dough into a 15-inch log. Sprinkle a cookie sheet with cornmeal. Place dough on cookie sheet and brush with some olive oil. Cover with plastic wrap and refrigerate overnight.

3. Remove from refrigerator, uncover, let stand at room temperature one hour. Make 3 diagonal cuts with a sharp knife.

4. Preheat oven to 425°F. Bake 25 to 30 minutes until golden brown. Remove from oven and cool on cake rack.

BAKE CYCLE: DOUGH

NUTRITIONAL INFORMATION PER SLICE	
Calories	104
Fat	.7 gram
Carbohydrate	209 grams
Protein	2.9 grams
Fiber	.8 gram
Sodium	233 milligrams
Cholesterol	1.1 milligrams

HERB ROLLS
✦✦✦

Such excellent rolls deserve a fine dinner. They go well with everything from prime roast beef to homemade chicken soup. (Note: If you make these ahead of time, cover to prevent them from turning hard.)

1½-POUND	1-POUND
4 tablespoons butter or margarine	3 tablespoons butter or margarine
3 tablespoons finely chopped onion	2 tablespoons finely chopped onion
1 large clove garlic, minced	1 medium clove garlic, minced
¾ teaspoon dried oregano	½ teaspoon dried oregano
¾ teaspoon dried basil	½ teaspoon dried basil
¾ teaspoon dried tarragon	½ teaspoon dried tarragon
1 cup water (for Welbilt/DAK and Zojirushi machines, add 2 tablespoons more water)	¾ cup water (for Welbilt machine, add 1 tablespoon more water)
3 cups all-purpose flour	2 cups all-purpose flour
1 teaspoon salt	1 teaspoon salt
1½ teaspoons sugar	1 teaspoon sugar
1½ teaspoons Red Star brand active dry yeast	1½ teaspoons Red Star brand active dry yeast

1. In a small skillet, melt the butter. Add onion, garlic, and herbs. Sauté over medium heat until onion is soft, about 5 minutes. Cool to room temperature.

2. Place all ingredients, including onion mixture, in bread pan, select Dough setting, and press Start.

3. When the dough has risen long enough, the machine will beep. Turn off bread machine, remove bread pan, and turn out dough onto a lightly floured countertop or cutting board.

4. Gently roll and stretch dough into an 18-inch rope. Grease a 12-cup muffin tin, a 9 × 13 × 2 inch pan, or a large baking sheet.

FOR 1½-POUND DOUGH

With a sharp knife, divide dough into 18 pieces. (Hint: First cut dough into 6 equal pieces, then cut each of those into three pieces.)

FOR 1-POUND DOUGH

With a sharp knife, divide dough into 12 pieces.

5. Roll dough into balls; place in prepared pan. Cover and let rise in a warm oven 30 to 45 minutes until doubled. (Hint: To warm oven slightly, turn oven on Warm setting for 1 minute, then turn it off, and place covered dough in oven to rise. Remove from oven to preheat.)

6. Preheat oven to 400°F. Bake 12 to 15 minutes until golden brown. Remove from oven and serve warm.

1½-pound dough yields 18 rolls
1-pound dough yields 12 rolls

BAKE CYCLE: DOUGH

NUTRITIONAL INFORMATION PER ROLL	
Calories	102
Fat	2.8 grams
Carbohydrate	16.5 grams
Protein	2.3 grams
Fiber	.7 gram
Sodium	141 milligrams
Cholesterol	6.9 milligrams

CHICKEN BROCCOLI POCKETS

✦✦✦

If you're lucky enough to have any of these left over, pop them in the freezer and you'll have a handy lunch to grab on those mornings you're running late for work. Reheat in a microwave oven for six to seven minutes on MEDIUM power.

1½-POUND

DOUGH

⅜ cup water (for Welbilt/DAK and Zojirushi machines, add 2 tablespoons more water)
⅝ cup milk
3 cups bread flour
1½ teaspoons salt
1½ tablespoons butter or margarine
3 tablespoons sugar
1½ teaspoons Red Star brand active dry yeast

FILLING

¾ cup cream of chicken soup
2 cups chopped, cooked chicken
2 cups frozen, chopped broccoli, thawed and drained
1 cup (4 ounces) grated Mozzarella cheese
¼ cup chopped onion

1-POUND

DOUGH

⅜ cup water (for Welbilt machine, add 1 tablespoon more water)
⅜ cup milk
2 cups bread flour
1 teaspoon salt
1 tablespoon butter or margarine
2 tablespoons sugar
1½ teaspoons Red Star brand active dry yeast

FILLING

⅔ cup cream of chicken soup
1⅓ cups chopped, cooked chicken
1⅓ cups frozen, chopped broccoli, thawed and drained
¾ cup (3 ounces) grated Mozzarella cheese
3 tablespoons chopped onion

1. Place dough ingredients in bread pan, select Dough setting, and press Start.

2. Meanwhile, in a medium bowl, combine the soup, chicken, broccoli, cheese, and onion; cover and refrigerate until needed.

3. When the dough has risen long enough, the machine will beep. Turn off bread machine, remove bread pan, and turn out dough onto a lightly floured countertop or cutting board. Shape dough into a log.

4. Grease a large baking sheet.

FOR 1½-POUND DOUGH

With a sharp knife, divide dough into 8 pieces.

FOR 1-POUND DOUGH

With a sharp knife, divide dough into 6 pieces.

5. With a rolling pin, roll each piece into a 6-inch circle. Place approximately ½ cup of filling on one side of circle and spread to within ½-inch of the edge. Fold other half of dough over filling. Seal well by pressing edges together with the tines of a fork. With same fork, prick top of each pocket a few times. Place pockets on prepared baking sheet.

6. Preheat oven to 375°F. Bake for 25 to 30 minutes until golden brown. Remove from oven and serve warm. Leftovers can be frozen.

1½-pound dough yields 8 pockets
1-pound dough yields 6 pockets

BAKE CYCLE: DOUGH

NUTRITIONAL INFORMATION PER POCKET	
Calories	371
Fat	11.3 grams
Carbohydrate	46.1 grams
Protein	20.5 grams
Fiber	2.9 grams
Sodium	738 milligrams
Cholesterol	52.8 milligrams

DAWN'S VANILLA RAISIN BREAD
❖❖❖

A student in one of our classes, Dawn Fletcher, gave us the idea of soaking raisins in vanilla, which inspired us to create this bread. As you can tell from the recipe, several alterations were necessary to make this loaf suitable for different machines. Take time to read through it carefully before you start. If you want to make this luscious bread on the spur of the moment, combine the raisins and the vanilla then microwave on HIGH for one minute, rather than soaking them for an hour. (Note: For a stronger vanilla flavor, reserve the vanilla drained from the raisins and use it as part of your liquid. If you plan to bake this bread often, use an inexpensive vanilla extract.)

1½-POUND LOAF

⅔ cup raisins soaked in 3 tablespoons vanilla for at least 1 hour then well drained

1⅛ cups buttermilk (for Welbilt/DAK machines, add 2 tablespoons more buttermilk; for the Zojirushi, no extra buttermilk is needed)

1 egg (for the Panasonic/National machine, omit the egg)

3½ cups bread flour

1 teaspoon salt

3 tablespoons butter or margarine

2 tablespoons sugar

2 teaspoons Red Star brand active dry yeast

1-POUND LOAF

½ cup raisins soaked in 2 tablespoons vanilla for at least 1 hour then well drained

¾ cup buttermilk (for Welbilt machine, no extra buttermilk is needed)

2 cups bread flour

¾ teaspoon salt

2 tablespoons butter or margarine (for the Welbilt, use 1 tablespoon butter)

1½ tablespoons sugar

1½ teaspoons Red Star brand active dry yeast

1. Drain raisins well. Place all ingredients in bread pan, select Light Crust setting, and press Start.

2. After the baking cycle ends, remove bread from pan, place on cake rack, and allow to cool 1 hour before slicing.

CRUST: LIGHT
OPTIONAL BAKE CYCLES:
    RAISIN/NUT
    SWEET BREAD

NUTRITIONAL INFORMATION
PER SLICE WITH EGG

Calories	180
Fat	3.3 grams
Carbohydrate	32.8 grams
Protein	4.7 grams
Fiber	1.4 grams
Sodium	200 milligrams
Cholesterol	22.6 milligrams

NUTRITIONAL INFORMATION
PER LOAF WITHOUT EGG

Calories	175
Fat	2.9 grams
Carbohydrate	32.8 grams
Protein	4.3 grams
Fiber	1.4 grams
Sodium	195 milligrams
Cholesterol	7.4 milligrams

SWEET MILK BREAD

✦✦✦

This is a wonderful, soft, finely textured white bread with a rich, sweet taste. Even served up plain, it's a very munchable bread.

1½-POUND LOAF

⅞ cup water (for Welbilt/DAK and Zojirushi machines, add 2 tablespoons more water)

½ cup sweetened condensed milk

3⅓ cups bread flour (for Welbilt/DAK machines, reduce the flour to 3 cups)

1 teaspoon salt

1 tablespoon butter or margarine

2 teaspoons Red Star brand active dry yeast

1-POUND LOAF

⅝ cup water (for Welbilt machine, no extra water is needed)

⅜ cup sweetened condensed milk

2 cups bread flour

1 teaspoon salt

1 tablespoon butter or margarine

1½ teaspoons Red Star brand active dry yeast

1. Place all ingredients in bread pan, select Light Crust setting, and press Start.

2. After the baking cycle ends, remove bread from pan, place on cake rack, and allow to cool 1 hour before slicing.

CRUST: LIGHT
OPTIONAL BAKE CYCLES:
SWEET BREAD
RAPID BAKE

NUTRITIONAL INFORMATION PER SLICE	
Calories	151
Fat	2.1 grams
Carbohydrate	28.4 grams
Protein	4 grams
Fiber	.9 gram
Sodium	174 milligrams
Cholesterol	5.9 milligrams

APPLESAUCE RYE BREAD
✦✦✦

The combination of applesauce, rye, and molasses makes for a moist, dark bread that's perfect for breakfast . . . a nice way to start the day.

1½-POUND LOAF

1 cup sweetened applesauce
¼ cup water (for Welbilt/DAK and Zojirushi machines, add 3 tablespoons more water)
2 tablespoons molasses
2¾ cups bread flour
1 cup rye flour
½ teaspoon salt
2 tablespoons butter or margarine
1 tablespoons caraway seeds
2 teaspoons Red Star brand active dry yeast

1-POUND LOAF

¾ cup sweetened applesauce
⅛ cup water (for Welbilt machine, no extra water is needed)
1½ tablespoons molasses
2 cups bread flour
½ cup rye flour
½ teaspoon salt
1½ tablespoons butter or margarine
2 teaspoons caraway seeds
1½ teaspoons Red Star brand active dry yeast

1. Place all ingredients in bread pan, select Light Crust setting, and press Start.

2. After the baking cycle ends, remove bread from pan, place on cake rack, and allow to cool 1 hour before slicing.

CRUST: LIGHT
OPTIONAL BAKE CYCLES:
   SWEET BREAD
   DELAYED TIMER

NUTRITIONAL INFORMATION
PER SLICE

Calories	153
Fat	2.1 grams
Carbohydrates	29.8 grams
Protein	3.5 grams
Fiber	2.2 grams
Sodium	92 milligrams
Cholesterol	4.4 milligrams

ANN'S BIEROCKS

◆◆◆

Ann Slaybaugh, Special Ed teacher and friend, often claimed she wasn't much of a cook. We found it hard to believe when she shared recipes like this one and also took to the bread machine like a pro! These buns are filled with hamburger, cabbage, cheese, and onion—perfect to have on hand for a light lunch or to take along on a camping trip. This basic recipe is fun to play with when you're in a creative mood.

1½-POUND	1-POUND
DOUGH	**DOUGH**
¾ cup water (for Welbilt/DAK and Zojirushi machines, add 2 tablespoons more water)	½ cup water (for Welbilt machine, add 1 tablespoon more water)
1 egg	1 egg
3 cups all-purpose flour	2 cups all-purpose flour
1 teaspoon salt	½ teaspoon salt
¼ cup oil	3 tablespoons oil
¼ cup sugar	3 tablespoons sugar
2 teaspoons Red Star brand active dry yeast	2 teaspoons Red Star brand active dry yeast
FILLING	**FILLING**
2 pounds ground beef	1½ pounds ground beef
¾ cup chopped onion	½ cup chopped onion
2 cups chopped cabbage	1½ cups chopped cabbage
Salt & pepper to taste	Salt & pepper to taste
¾ cup (3 ounces) grated Cheddar cheese	½ cup (2 ounces) grated Cheddar cheese
2 tablespoons melted butter or margarine	2 tablespoons melted butter or margarine

1. Place dough ingredients in bread pan, select Dough setting, and press Start.

2. Meanwhile, in a medium skillet, brown the meat. Drain off all grease. Return skillet to heat and add the onion, cabbage, salt and pepper. Cover and cook on low heat for 15 minutes until the cabbage is tender. Stir in the cheese. Remove mixture from heat and set aside.

3. When the dough has risen long enough, the machine will beep. Turn off bread machine, remove bread pan, and turn out dough onto a lightly floured countertop or cutting board. Gently roll and stretch dough into a 12-inch rope.

FOR 1½-POUND DOUGH

With a sharp knife, divide the dough into 16 pieces.

FOR 1-POUND DOUGH

With a sharp knife, divide the dough into 12 pieces.

4. Grease a large baking sheet.

5. With a rolling pin, roll each piece into a 5-inch circle. Place a heaping ¼ cup of filling mixture in the center of each circle. Pull the edges up to meet in the center and pinch the dough together well to seal. Place on prepared baking sheet, sealed side down. Cover and let rise in warm oven 20 minutes until doubled. (Hint: To warm oven slightly, turn oven on Warm setting for 1 minute, then turn it off, and place covered dough in oven to rise. Remove from oven to preheat.) Remove baking sheet from oven then preheat oven to 350°F.

6. Before baking, brush each bun with the melted butter. Bake 20 minutes until golden brown. Remove from oven and serve warm.

1½-pound dough yields 16 buns
1-pound dough yields 12 buns

BAKE CYCLE: DOUGH

NUTRITIONAL INFORMATION PER BUN	
Calories	335
Fat	19.1 grams
Carbohydrate	22.2 grams
Protein	17.8 grams
Fiber	1.1 grams
Sodium	231 milligrams
Cholesterol	73.5 milligrams

SHAREEN'S WHOLE WHEAT PIZZA CRUST
✦✦✦

When the other cheerleaders are tossing little Shareen in the air, I wonder if she's thinking about this whole wheat pizza crust. Probably not. More likely she's just contemplating her landing. However, we think of it often when the idea of having pizza for dinner comes to mind. We found this whole wheat crust added a new dimension to our homemade pizzas . . . a delightful "earthy" flavor.

1½-POUND	1-POUND
1 cup water (for Welbilt/DAK and Zojirushi machines, add 2 tablespoons more water)	¾ cup water (for Welbilt machine, add 1 tablespoon more water)
3 cups whole wheat flour	2 cups whole wheat flour
1 teaspoon salt	1 teaspoon salt
2 tablespoons olive oil	1½ tablespoons olive oil
1½ teaspoons sugar	1 teaspoon sugar
1½ teaspoons Red Star brand active dry yeast	1½ teaspoons Red Star brand active dry yeast

1. Place dough ingredients in bread pan, select Dough setting, and press Start.

2. When the dough has risen long enough, the machine will beep. Turn off bread machine, remove bread pan, and turn out dough onto a lightly floured countertop or cutting board. Form dough into a mound and allow it to rest for 10 minutes.

FOR 1½-POUND DOUGH

Grease one deep-dish or two 12- or 14-inch pizza pans. With your hands, gently stretch and press dough to fit evenly into pan(s). For the deep dish pan, press the dough halfway up the sides of the pan.

FOR 1-POUND DOUGH

Grease one 14-inch pizza pan. With your hands, gently stretch and press dough to fit evenly into pan.

3. Spread your favorite pizza sauce on top of the dough, then add toppings of your choice, except cheese.

4. Preheat oven to 450°F. Bake for 15 to 20 minutes. Sprinkle cheese on top of hot pizza as soon as you remove it from the oven. Serve hot.

1½-pound dough yields one deep-dish pizza or two 12- or 14-inch pizzas. 1-pound dough yields one 14-inch pizza

MENU SELECTION: DOUGH

NUTRITIONAL INFORMATION FOR 1½-POUND DOUGH	
Calories	1494
Fat	33.8 grams
Carbohydrates	268 grams
Protein	50.5 grams
Fiber	46.5 grams
Sodium	2159 milligrams
Cholesterol	0 milligrams

NUTRITIONAL INFORMATION FOR 1-POUND DOUGH	
Calories	1019
Fat	24.8 grams
Carbohydrates	178 grams
Protein	34.1 grams
Fiber	31.4 grams
Sodium	2151 milligrams
Cholesterol	0 milligrams

OATMEAL BREAD
◆◆◆

This bakes up into a gorgeous, tall loaf in most machines and has an unmistakable wholesome, oatmeal flavor. It's a wonderful sandwich bread.

1½-POUND LOAF

1 cup old-fashioned rolled oats
1⅜ cups buttermilk (for Welbilt/DAK and Zojirushi machines, add 3 tablespoons more buttermilk)
3 tablespoons honey
3 cups bread flour
1½ teaspoons salt
2 tablespoons butter or margarine
2 teaspoons Red Star brand active dry yeast

1-POUND LOAF

⅔ cup old-fashioned rolled oats
⅞ cup buttermilk (for Welbilt machine, add 1 tablespoon more buttermilk)
2 tablespoons honey
2 cups bread flour
1 teaspoon salt
1½ tablespoons butter or margarine
1½ teaspoons Red Star brand active dry yeast

1. Place all ingredients in bread pan, select Light Crust setting, and press Start.

2. After the baking cycle ends, remove bread from pan, place on cake rack, and allow to cool 1 hour before slicing.

CRUST: LIGHT
OPTIONAL BAKE CYCLES:
SWEET BREAD
RAPID BAKE

NUTRITIONAL INFORMATION PER SLICE	
Calories	159
Fat	2.5 grams
Carbohydrates	29.2 grams
Protein	4.7 grams
Fiber	1.5 grams
Sodium	269 milligrams
Cholesterol	5.3 milligrams

DENNIS'S MULTIGRAIN BREAD

❖❖❖

Dennis, Linda's husband, raves about this bread every time he has a slice, so it was fitting to name it after him. Any multigrain cereal—four-, seven-, nine-, or twelve-grain—may be used in this full-bodied bread. Arrowhead Mills and Stonebuhr are two companies that produce and package this coarse-meal cereal. Do not use the version sold in grocery stores that resembles cornflakes.

1½-POUND LOAF

¾ cup buttermilk
⅜ cup water (for Welbilt/DAK
   and Zojirushi machines, add 2
   tablespoons more water)
1 egg
2 tablespoons oil
2 tablespoons honey
2½ cups whole wheat flour
½ cup multigrain cereal
1½ teaspoons salt
¼ cup raw, unsalted sunflower
   seeds
3 tablespoons gluten
2 teaspoons Red Star brand
   active dry yeast

1-POUND LOAF

⅜ cup buttermilk
⅛ cup water (for Welbilt
   machine, no extra water is
   needed)
1 egg
1½ tablespoons oil
1½ tablespoons honey
1⅔ cups whole wheat flour
⅓ cup multigrain cereal
1 teaspoon salt
3 tablespoons raw, unsalted
   sunflower seeds
2 tablespoons gluten
2 teaspoons Red Star brand
   active dry yeast

1. Place all ingredients in bread pan, select Light Crust setting, and press Start.

2. After the baking cycle ends, remove bread from pan, place on cake rack, and allow to cool 1 hour before slicing.

CRUST: LIGHT	
OPTIONAL BAKE CYCLES:	
WHOLE WHEAT	
RAISIN/NUT	

NUTRITIONAL INFORMATION PER SLICE	
Calories	143
Fat	4.2 grams
Carbohydrate	22.5 grams
Protein	5.8 grams
Fiber	3.1 grams
Sodium	248 milligrams
Cholesterol	15.7 milligrams

HAM AND PEPPER CHEESE BREAD
❖❖❖

Perk up your spirits and your taste buds some gloomy day with this spicy sandwich loaf. It freezes well and can be microwaved for a quick lunch. If you prefer, use sliced turkey or roast beef instead of ham. Let your imagination be your guide with this one.

1½-POUND

DOUGH

½ cup milk
⅜ cup water (for Welbilt/DAK and Zojirushi machines, add 2 tablespoons more water)
1 egg
3 cups bread flour
3 tablespoons wheat germ
2 tablespoons instant potato flakes
1½ teaspoons salt
1½ tablespoons oil
3 tablespoons sugar
1½ teaspoons Red Star brand active dry yeast

FILLING

8 thin slices ham
1½ cups (6 ounces) grated Cheddar cheese
1½ cups (6 ounces) grated jalapeño pepper cheese

1-POUND

DOUGH

⅜ cup milk
¼ cup water (for Welbilt machine, add 1 tablespoon more water)
1 egg
2 cups bread flour
2 tablespoons wheat germ
1 tablespoon instant potato flakes
1 teaspoon salt
1 tablespoon oil
2 tablespoons sugar
1½ teaspoons Red Star brand active dry yeast

FILLING

6 thin slices ham
1 cup (4 ounces) grated Cheddar cheese
1 cup (4 ounces) grated jalapeño pepper cheese

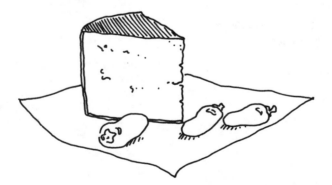

1. Place dough ingredients in bread pan, select Dough setting, and press Start.

2. When the dough has risen long enough, the machine will beep. Turn off bread machine, remove bread pan, and turn out dough onto a lightly floured countertop or cutting board.

FOR 1½-POUND DOUGH

With a rolling pin, roll dough into a 12 × 21 inch rectangle.

FOR 1-POUND DOUGH

With a rolling pin, roll dough into a 10 × 15 inch rectangle.

3. Grease a large baking sheet. Preheat oven to 350°F.

4. Cover dough with ham and sprinkle cheeses on top. Starting at long edge, roll up tightly; pinch seam and ends to seal. Place seam side down on prepared baking sheet.

5. Bake for 30 minutes until brown. Remove from oven and allow to cool for 2 minutes. Slice into 3-inch-wide pieces. Serve warm.

1½-pound dough yields 7 sandwiches
1-pound dough yields 5 sandwiches

BAKE CYCLE: DOUGH

NUTRITIONAL INFORMATION PER SANDWICH	
Calories	246
Fat	8.8 grams
Carbohydrate	30.2 grams
Protein	10.9 grams
Fiber	1.2 grams
Sodium	575 milligrams
Cholesterol	39.7 milligrams

COUNTRY RYE BREAD STICKS
✦✦✦

They may be funny looking but these mild rye bread sticks taste mighty fine.

1½-POUND	1-POUND
1 cup water (for Welbilt/DAK and Zojirushi machines, add 2 tablespoons more water)	¾ cup water (for Welbilt machine, add 1 tablespoon more water)
1½ cups bread flour	1 cup bread flour
1 cup rye flour	⅔ cup rye flour
½ cup whole wheat flour	⅓ cup whole wheat flour
½ teaspoon salt	½ teaspoon salt
2 tablespoons butter or margarine	1½ tablespoons butter or margarine
2 tablespoons sugar	1½ tablespoons sugar
2 teaspoons caraway seeds	1 teaspoon caraway seeds
1½ teaspoons Red Star brand active dry yeast	1½ teaspoons Red Star brand active dry yeast

1. Place dough ingredients in bread pan, select Dough setting, and press Start.

2. When the dough has risen long enough, the machine will beep. Turn off bread machine, remove bread pan, and turn out dough onto a lightly floured countertop or cutting board. Shape dough into 6-inch square.

3. Grease two 12 × 16 × 1 inch baking sheets. Preheat oven to 350°F.

FOR 1½-POUND DOUGH

With a very sharp knife, divide dough into 32 strips. (Hint: First cut dough lengthwise into 4 equal pieces, then cut each piece lengthwise into 8 thin strips.)

FOR 1-POUND DOUGH

With a very sharp knife, divide dough into 24 strips. (Hint: First cut dough lengthwise into 4 equal pieces then cut each piece lengthwise into 6 thin strips.)

4. Roll and stretch each piece into a 16-inch-long stick; place on prepared baking sheet.

5. Bake for 20 to 25 minutes. Remove from oven; remove bread sticks from pans and cool on wire racks. Once cool, store at room temperature in plastic bags. They will stay fresh for 3 or 4 days.

1½-pound dough yields 32 bread sticks
1-pound dough yields 24 bread sticks

BAKE CYCLE: DOUGH

NUTRITIONAL INFORMATION PER BREAD STICK	
Calories	50
Fat	.9 gram
Carbohydrate	9.2 grams
Protein	1.2 grams
Fiber	.9 gram
Sodium	40 milligrams
Cholesterol	1.9 milligrams

CHRISTY'S CHRISTMAS TREES
✦✦✦

This is a scrumptious coffee cake that even young children can take part in creating. It's a thoughtful gift during the holiday season, perfect for breakfast Christmas morning or for a Christmas Eve family gathering.

1½-POUND

DOUGH

⅞ cup buttermilk (for Welbilt/DAK and Zojirushi machines, add 2 tablespoons more buttermilk)
1 egg
3 cups all-purpose flour
1 teaspoon salt
4 tablespoons butter or margarine
¼ cup sugar
1½ teaspoons Red Star brand active dry yeast

ICING

1 cup powdered sugar
1 to 1½ tablespoons milk or eggnog
½ teaspoon vanilla

Green food coloring

GARNISH

Cinnamon red hot candies

1-POUND

DOUGH

⅝ cup buttermilk (for Welbilt machine, add 1 tablespoon more water)
1 egg
2 cups all-purpose flour
1 teaspoon salt
3 tablespoons butter or margarine
3 tablespoons sugar
1½ teaspoons Red Star brand active dry yeast

ICING

⅔ cup powdered sugar
2 to 3 teaspoons milk or eggnog
¼ teaspoon vanilla

Green food coloring

GARNISH

Cinnamon red hot candies

1. Place dough ingredients in bread pan, select Dough setting, and press Start.

2. When the dough has risen long enough, the machine will beep. Turn off bread machine, remove bread pan, and turn out dough onto a lightly floured countertop or cutting board. Gently roll and stretch dough into an 18-inch rope. Grease a large baking sheet(s).

FOR 1½-POUND DOUGH

With a sharp knife, divide the dough into 17 pieces. Roll each piece into a ball and place it on the greased baking sheet in the shape of a Christmas tree,

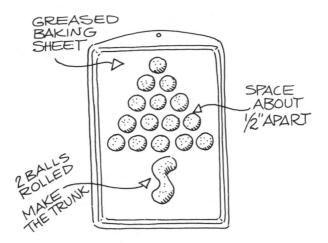

GREASED
BAKING
SHEET

SPACE
ABOUT
½"APART

2 BALLS
ROLLED
MAKE
THE TRUNK

spaced about a half-inch apart: 5 balls for the bottom row, 4 balls for the next row, 3 balls for the next row, 2 balls for the next row, and 1 ball at the top. Combine the remaining 2 balls into 1 large ball, gently roll it into a thick rope and shape it into an "S" to form the tree trunk.

VARIATION:

This recipe makes one large Christmas tree coffee cake. To create 2, 4, or 6 smaller trees, simply divide the dough into 2, 4, or 6 pieces initially and then follow the directions for dividing up the dough and shaping each tree.

FOR 1-POUND DOUGH

With a sharp knife, divide the dough into 11 pieces. Roll each piece into a ball and place it on the greased baking sheet in the shape of a tree, spaced about a half-inch apart: 4 balls for the bottom row, 3 balls for the next row, 2 balls for the next row, and 1 ball at the top. Gently roll the remaining ball into a thick rope and shape it into an "S" to form the tree trunk.

VARIATION:

This recipe makes one medium Christmas tree coffee cake. To create 2 or 4 smaller trees, simply divide the dough into 2 or 4 pieces initially and then follow the directions for dividing up the dough and shaping each tree.

3. Cover and let rise in a warm oven for 30 to 45 minutes until doubled. (Hint: To warm oven slightly, turn oven on Warm setting for 1 minute, then turn it off, and place covered dough in oven to rise. Remove from oven to preheat.) Remove baking sheet(s) from oven. Preheat oven to 375°F.

4. Bake 20 to 25 minutes until golden. Cool on a cake rack.

5. When the coffee cake(s) is cooled, in a small bowl, combine the icing ingredients, adding enough liquid to make the icing thin enough to spread over the coffee cake. Spread each roll with icing, then decorate with cinnamon red hot candies.

Yields 1 Christmas tree coffee cake

BAKE CYCLE: DOUGH

NUTRITIONAL INFORMATION PER CHRISTMAS TREE	
Calories	149
Fat	3.4 grams
Carbohydrate	26.3 grams
Protein	3.2 grams
Fiber	.7 gram
Sodium	166 milligrams
Cholesterol	20.5 milligrams

SOUR RYE BREAD
◆◆◆

We think this combination of sour cream and rye is a winner. This slightly tangy loaf baked up quite differently from machine to machine. In some it was a real dome thumper, in others it needed added gluten. Try it the first time without adding extra gluten. If necessary add gluten to future loaves if the trial loaf baked up small.

1½-POUND LOAF

⅞ cup water (for Welbilt/DAK and Zojirushi machines, add 1 tablespoon more water)
½ cup sour cream
2¼ cups bread flour
1 cup rye flour
1½ teaspoons salt
2 tablespoons sugar
1 tablespoon caraway seeds
3 tablespoons gluten, optional
2 teaspoons Red Star brand active dry yeast

1-POUND LOAF

⅝ cup water (for Welbilt machine, add 1 tablespoon more water)
¼ cup sour cream
1⅓ cups bread flour
⅔ cup rye flour
1 teaspoon salt
1½ tablespoons sugar
2 teaspoons caraway seeds
2 tablespoons gluten, optional
1½ teaspoons Red Star brand active dry yeast

1. Place all ingredients in bread pan, select Light Crust setting, and press Start.

2. After the baking cycle ends, remove bread from pan, place on cake rack, and allow to cool 1 hour before slicing.

CRUST: LIGHT

NUTRITIONAL INFORMATION PER SLICE	
Calories	134
Fat	2.2 grams
Carbohydrates	24.2 grams
Protein	4 grams
Fiber	1.8 grams
Sodium	234 milligrams
Cholesterol	3.6 milligrams

Suggested Uses

✦✦✦

We've had several requests to include this section again. These suggestions might help you select which bread to give as a gift, which to take to a potluck supper, etc.

SANDWICH BREADS

Applesauce Rye Bread
Buttermilk Honey Bran Bread
DeDe's Buttermilk Bread
Dennis's Multigrain Bread
French Bread Extraordinaire!
Lois's Country Crunch Bread

Oatmeal Bread
Quaker Multigrain Bread
Sour Rye Bread
Sweet Milk Bread
Whole Wheat Hamburger and Hot
   Dog Buns

BREAKFAST BREADS OR TOAST

Anne and Bill's Apple Oatmeal Bread
   with Raisins
Applesauce Rye Bread
Christy's Christmas Trees
Dawn's Vanilla Raisin Bread
Dennis's Multigrain Bread
Jana's Seed and Nut Bread
Jim's Cinnamon Rolls

Jim's Maple Walnut Bread
Linda's Lemon Bread
Oatmeal Bread
San Diego Sunshine Bread
Sour Rye Bread
Sweet Lelani Bread
Whole Wheat Cinnamon Raisin
   Bread

SNACKING BREADS

Anne and Bill's Apple Oatmeal Bread
   with Raisins
Country Rye Bread Sticks
Dawn's Vanilla Raisin Bread
Dennis's Multigrain Bread
Herb Bread
Jana's Seed and Nut Bread
Jim's Maple Walnut Bread

Linda's Lemon Bread
Oatmeal Bread
San Diego Sunshine Bread
Sour Rye Bread
Sweet Lelani Bread
Sweet Milk Bread
Whole Wheat Cinnamon Raisin
   Bread

GIFT BREADS

Anne and Bill's Apple Oatmeal Bread
  with Raisins
Christy's Christmas Trees
Country Rye Bread Sticks
Dawn's Vanilla Raisin Bread
DeDe's Buttermilk Bread
Dennis's Multigrain Bread
French Bread Extraordinaire!
Jalapeño Cheese Bread
Jana's Seed and Nut Bread
Jim's Cinnamon Rolls
Jim's Maple Walnut Bread

Linda's Lemon Bread
Lois's Country Crunch Bread
Oatmeal Bread
San Diego Sunshine Bread
Sour Rye Bread
Sweet Lelani Bread
Sweet Milk Bread
Whole Wheat Cinnamon Raisin
  Bread
Whole Wheat Hamburger and Hot
  Dog Buns

DINNER PARTY BREADS

Ann's Bierocks
Buttermilk Honey Bran Bread
Chicken Broccoli Pockets
Country Rye Bread Sticks
French Bread Extraordinaire!
Ham and Pepper Cheese Bread
Herb Bread
Herb Rolls
Jalapeño Cheese Bread

Jana's Seed and Nut Bread
Linda's Lemon Bread
Lois's Country Crunch Bread
Oatmeal Bread
Quaker Multigrain Bread
Shareen's Whole Wheat Pizza Crust
Shayna's Vegan Burgers
Sour Rye Bread

STUFFING/CROUTONS/BREAD CRUMBS

Applesauce Rye Bread
Buttermilk Honey Bran Bread
Dennis's Multigrain Bread
Herb Bread
Jalapeño Cheese Bread

Linda's Lemon Bread
Lois's Country Crunch Bread
Oatmeal Bread
Quaker Multigrain Bread
Sour Rye Bread

MOST AROMATIC BREADS

Dawn's Vanilla Raisin Bread
Herb Bread
Jalapeño Cheese Bread
Linda's Lemon Bread

San Diego Sunshine Bread
Whole Wheat Cinnamon Raisin
  Bread

BREADS THAT CAN BE BAKED ON THE DELAYED TIMER

Anne and Bill's Apple Oatmeal
  Bread with Raisins
Applesauce Rye Bread

Lois's Country Crunch Bread
San Diego Sunshine Bread

✦✦✦ 7 ✦✦✦

Sources

INGREDIENTS

Universal Foods Corporation
433 East Michigan Street
P.O. Box 737
Milwaukee, WI 53201
1-800-445-4746

Red Star Active Dry Yeast, Quick Rise Yeast, and Instant Yeast in bulk packages

Bob's Red Mill
Natural Foods, Inc.
5209 S.E. International Way
Milwaukie, OR 97222
1-800-553-2258

A wide variety of specialty grains, cereals, and flours including stone-ground whole wheat bread flour; wheat berries for hand grinding; lecithin; whey; diastatic malt; plus xanthan gum and gluten-free flours (Catalog)

Ener-G Foods, Inc.
P.O. Box 84487
Seattle, WA 98124-5787
1-800-331-5222 (outside WA)
1-800-325-9788 (in WA)

Dietetic specialty foods: soyquik (replaces instant nonfat dry milk); egg replacer; gluten-free flours; wheat-free and gluten-free bread machine mixes; methocel, xanthan gum; guar gum

King Arthur Flour
RR 2, Box 56
Norwich, VT 05055
1-800-827-6836

Various flours including white whole wheat flour; diastatic malt; xanthan gum; gluten-free flours; Fruit Sweet 100% refined-sugar-free sweetener, plastic bread bags for large loaves and baguettes; caramel coloring for dark rye breads; baking stones and peels; baguette pans (Catalog)

Dietary Specialties, Inc.
P.O. Box 227
Rochester, NY 14601
1-716-263-2787

Dietetic specialty foods including gluten-free flours, xanthan gum, flavoring extracts with non-grain alcohol, non-dairy powdered milk substitutes

Tad Enterprises
9356 Pleasant
Tinley Park, IL 60477
1-800-438-6153

Dietetic specialty products including gluten-free flours, tapioca and potato starch, xanthan gum

Jaffe Bros.
P.O. Box 636-Z
Valley Center, CA 92082-0636
1-619-749-1133

Flours, grains, dried fruits, nuts, seeds, wheat and rye berries, hulled barley (Catalog)

Magic Mill
1515 South 400 West
Salt Lake City, UT 84115-5110
1-800-888-8587

Dough enhancer, gluten, Saf instant yeast, hard red wheat berries, white winter wheat berries, bread machine mixes, bread machines (Hitachi, Maxim, Panasonic), electric and manual grain mills, dehydrators (Catalog)

Walnut Acres
Penns Creek, PA 17862
1-800-433-3998

Organic flours, grains, cereals, dried fruits, nuts, herbs and spices (Catalog)

Saco Buttermilk Powder
P.O. Box 5461
Madison, WI 53705
1-800-373-SACO

Dried buttermilk powder

J. B. Dough & Company
200 Paw Paw Avenue
Benton Harbor, MI 49022-3400
1-800-528-6222

A large assortment of bread machine mixes, including a sampler pack (Catalog)

EQUIPMENT AND ACCESSORIES

Chef's Catalog
3215 Commercial Avenue
Northbrook, IL 60062-1900
1-800-338-3232

Professional restaurant equipment for the home chef: Panasonic bread machines, French bread pans, bread box, kitchen towels, knives, necklace timers (Catalog)

Community Kitchens
P.O. Box 2311, Dept JM
Baton Rouge, LA 70821-2311
1-800-535-9901

Fiddlebow knife, crumb box cutting board, Panasonic bread machines, packaged bread mixes, perforated French bread pans, bread box, set of measuring cups in $\frac{1}{4}$-, $\frac{1}{3}$-, $\frac{1}{2}$-, $\frac{2}{3}$-, $\frac{3}{4}$-, and 1-cup sizes (Catalog)

DAK Industries, Inc.
8200 Remmet Avenue
Canoga Park, CA 91304
1-800-DAK-0800
1-800-888-6703 (TDD—hearing
   impaired number)

DAK bread machines, a bread holder for cutting round loaves into uniform slices, an electric snack/sandwich maker for round bread slices (Catalog)

Delta Rehabilitation, Inc.
411 Bryn Mawr Island
Bradenton, FL 34207
1-813-758-9093
Contact: Irwin Franzel

Zojirush S-15 bread machine, Back to Basics hand grain mill, Jupiter electric grain mill

Jessica's Biscuit
Box 301
Newtonville, MA 02160
1-800-878-4264

Specialty cookbooks from dozens of publishers (Catalog)

Lillian Vernon
Virginia Beach, VA 23479-0002
1-804-430-5555

Bread board with crumb tray, pizza stone (Catalog)

Miles Kimball
41 West Eighth Ave.
Oshkosh, WI 54906-0002

Personalized paper bread bags (Catalog)

The Wooden Spoon
P.O. Box 931
Clinton, CT 06413-0931
1-800-431-2207

Fiddle-bow bread knife, bread board with crumb tray, baking stone and peel, dehydrator, citrus zester (Catalog)

RESOURCES

Bailey, Janet. *Keeping Food Fresh.* New York: Harper and Row, 1989.

Beard, James. *Beard on Bread.* New York: Ballantine Books, 1973.

Better Homes and Gardens. *Complete Guide to Food and Cooking.* Des Moines, IA: Meredith Corp., 1991.

Brody, Jane. *Jane Brody's Good Food Book.* New York: W. W. Norton & Co., 1985.

————. *Jane Brody's Nutrition Book*. New York: W. W. Norton & Co., 1981.

————. *The New York Times Guide to Personal Health*. New York: Times Books, 1982.

Clayton, Jr., Bernard. *Bernard Clayton's New Complete Book of Breads*. New York: Simon & Schuster, 1987.

Dworkin, Floss, and Stan Dworkin. *Bake Your Own Bread*. New York: Plume, 1987.

Eckhardt, Linda West, and Diana Collingwood Butts. *Bread in Half the Time*. New York: Crown Publishers, 1991.

Hittner, Patricia. "The New Food Additives: Can They Really Deliver Flavor Without Guilt?," *Better Homes and Gardens*, April 1992.

Jones, Judith, and Evan Jones. *The Book of Bread*. New York: Harper & Row, 1982.

Kilham, Christopher S. *The Bread and Circus Whole Food Bible*. Reading, MA: Addison-Wesley Publishing Co., 1991.

Manning, Elise W. *Farm Journal's Complete Home Baking Book*. Garden City, NY: Doubleday & Co., 1979.

Mindell, Earl. *Vitamin Bible*. New York: Warner Books, 1979.

McGee, Harold. *On Food and Cooking: The Science and Lore of the Kitchen*. New York: Collier Books, 1984.

Moore, Ken. *Bread Baking: Problems and Their Solutions*. Ukiah, CA: Moore Publishing, 1991.

Moore, Marilyn M. *The Wooden Spoon Bread Book*. New York: The Atlantic Monthly Press, 1987.

Ojakangas, Beatrice. *Great Whole-Grain Breads*. New York: Dutton, 1984.

Pappas, Lou Seibert. *Bread Baking*. San Leandro, CA: Bristol Publishing, 1992.

"Quinoa, The Healthful Grain." *Better Homes and Gardens*, December 1992.

Robertson, Laurel. *The Laurel's Kitchen Bread Book*. New York: Random House, 1984.

Rombauer, Irma S., and Marion Rombauer Becker. *Joy of Cooking*. New York: Bobbs-Merrill Co., 1975.

Index

A

Accessories and equipment extras,
 134–138
 sources for, 191–192
Active dry yeast, 67
Adapting recipes to bread machine,
 114–115
Air bubbles, preventing, 128
All-purpose flour, 50
Amaranth, 64
Amaranth flour, 55
Animal products, breads without, 102–103
Anne and Bill's Apple Oatmeal Bread with
 Raisins, 143
Ann's Bierocks, 172–173
Apple oatmeal bread with raisins,
 143
Apples, 91
Applesauce Rye Bread, 171
Aromatic breads, 188
Ascorbic acid, 51, 83

B

Baking bread, 42–43, 110–111
Baking sheets, 136
Bananas, 88
Barley, 63

Barley flour, 55
 malted, 81–82, 100, 103
Barley malt syrup, 78, 99, 103
Beer, 72
Bibliography, 192–193
Bierocks, 172–173
Blisters on top, preventing, 129
Bob's Cheddar Cheese Bread (gluten-free),
 107
Bob's Red Mill, 190
Books, 192–193
Bran, 59, 62–63
Bread-baking facts and guidelines 39–48
 baking, 42–43
 delayed bake timer, 5–6, 46–47, 188
 helpful hints, 109–120
 ingredients, 40, 43
 judging dough, 44–46
 measurements/conversions, 47–48
 measuring ingredients, 44
 mixing/kneading dough, 40
 rising of dough, 40–42
 weather and bread, 46, 118–119
 See also Ingredients
Bread crumbs, breads for, 188
Bread flour, 49, 51
 substitutions for, 90
Bread machine baking, guidelines, 43–48
 delayed bake timer, 5–6, 46–47, 188
 helpful hints, 109–120

Bread machine baking (cont.)
  ingredients, 43
  judging dough, 44–46
  measurements/conversions, 47–48
  measuring ingredients, 44
  troubleshooting techniques, 113,
    120–131
  weather and, 46, 118–119
  See also Ingredients; Recipes
Bread machine cleaning, 133–134
Bread machine features, 1–6
  cool-down cycle, 5
  crust color selection, 5–6
  delayed bake timer, 5–6, 46–47, 188
  dough cycle, 3, 111
  french bread cycle, 4
  jam/rice/cakes/quick breads, 4–5
  loaf shape, 2–3
  loaf size, 2
  power saver, 6
  preheat cycle, 3
  raisin/nut cycle, 4, 112
  rapid bake cycle, 3
  sweet bread cycle, 4
  viewing window, 5
  whole wheat cycle, 4
  yeast dispenser, 6
Bread machine models, 7–38
  Dak, 7–9
  Hitachi, 10–12
  MK Seiko, 13–16
  Maxim, 17
  Panasonic/National, 18–20
  Regal, 21–23
  Sanyo, 24–25
  Toastmaster, 26–27
  Trillium, 28
  Welbilt, 29–34
  West Bend, 35–36
  Zojirushi, 37–38
Bread machine recipes
  adapting your own to, 114–115
  creating, 116–117
  gluten-free 106–108
  See also Recipes
Breakfast breads, 186
Brewer's yeast, 65
Bromated flour, 51, 83
Brown rice syrup, 78, 99

Brown sugar, 74
Brown and white bread (gluten-free), 108
Buckwheat flour, 55
Buckwheat groats, 63–64
Bulgur, 60
Bulletin boards, computer, 113–114
Burnt crusts, 128
Butter, 72, 91
  reducing or eliminating, 97–98
Buttermilk, 71, 88
  substitutions for, 99–91
Buttermilk bread, 142
Buttermilk Honey Bran Bread, 154

C

Cake flour, 51
Cake yeast, 68
Cakes, 4–5
Caldwell, Linda, 138
Caramel coloring, 87
Cason, Jana, 41
Celiac Spruce Association/USA, 105
Cheese, 88. See also Dairy products
Cheddar cheese bread (gluten-free), 107
Cheese breads, 107, 151, 178–179
Chef's Catalog, 191
Chicken Broccoli Pockets, 166–167
Chili peppers, 87–88
Cholesterol, lowering, 98–99
Christy's Christmas Trees, 182–184
Cinnamon raisin bread (whole wheat), 161
Cinnamon rolls, 146–147
Citrus fruit, 89. See also Zest
Cleaning your machine, 133–134
Climatic conditions, bread and, 46,
    118–119
Coarse, crumbly texture, preventing, 130
Coarse, holey-textured bread, preventing,
    129
Coffee cake, Christmas, 182–184
Collapsed sides, preventing, 129
Commercial dough enhancers, 83
Community Kitchens, 191
Compressed (fresh) yeast, 68
Computer bulletin boards, 113–114
Conversions/measurements, 47–48
Cooking Echo, The, 113

Cool-down cycle, 5
Corn flour and cornmeal, 57, 63
Corn syrup, 77
Cost of bread machines, 2
Country crunch bread, 162–163
Country Rye Bread Sticks, 180–181
Cracked wheat, 60
Cracked whole rye, 61
Cracks, preventing, 127
Creating your own recipes, 116–117
Crisp crusts, 129
Croutons, breads for, 144, 188
Crumbly texture, preventing, 130
Crust color selection, 5–6
Crusts problems, preventing
    burnt, 128
    crisp, 129
    soft, 128
    tough, 128

D

Dairy products, 88
    breads without, 102–103
    See also Milk
DAK Industries, Inc., 192
    Auto Bakery, 7
    Turbo Baker II, 8
    Turbo Baker IV, 9
Date sugar, 75
Dawn's Vanilla Raisin Bread, 168–169
Dede's Buttermilk Bread, 142
Dehydrator, 136
Delayed bake timer
    breads for, 188
    description of, 5
    guidelines for using, 46–47
    yeast dispenser and, 6
Delta Rehabilitation, 192
Dennis's Multigrain Bread, 177
Dental floss, 136
Diastatic malt powder, 81–82, 100,
    103
Dietary needs, adjusting recipes for,
    95–108
Dietary Specialties, 190
Dinner party breads, 187
Dirty machines, cleaning, 133–134

Dough
    freezing, 132
    judging, 44–46
    refrigerating, 131
Dough cycle, 3, 111
Dough enhancers, 81–83
    ascorbic acid, 51, 83
    commercial dough enhancers, 83
    gluten, 81
    lecithin, 82
    malt powder, 81–82
    potassium bromate, 51, 83
Dough scraper, 135
Dried fruits, 88, 90
Dry bread, preventing, 129–130
Durum flour, 53

E

Eggs, 78–79
    substitutions, 91, 97–98, 103
Electric snackmaker, 136
Ener-G Foods, 91, 98, 103–105, 190
Equipment and accessories
    extras, 134–138
    sources for, 191–192

F

Fast-acting yeasts, 67–68
Fats, 72–73
    reducing or eliminating, 97–98
    substitutions, 91
Fermentation process, 66–67
Fiber, maximizing, 101–102
Fidonet, 113
Flour, 40
    gluten-free, 56–57
    non-wheat, 54–55
    wheat, 49–53
    whole grain, 58–65
Franzel, Irwin, 120
Freezing
    bread, 138
    buttermilk, 71
    dough, 131–132
    yeast, 68

French baguette pans, 136–137
French bread cycle, 4
French Bread Extraordinaire!, 158–159
Fresh (compressed) yeast, 68
Fructose, 75, 99
Fruit, 88–89
    reducing or eliminating fats with, 97
    substitutions, 91
Fruit juice sweeteners, 78, 99
Fruit Source, 78, 99
Fruit Sweet, 78, 99

G

Gene's Basic Rice Bread (gluten-free), 106
Gift breads, 187
Gluten, 40, 79–81
Gluten-free breads, 104–108
    recipes, 106–108
Gluten-free flours and grains, 56–57
    corn, 57, 63
    legume, 57
    potato, 56
    quinoa, 57, 64
    rice, 56
    soy, 56–57
    storage of, 57
    tapioca, 57
Graham flour, 53
Granulated white sugar, 74
Guar gum, 104

H

Ham and Pepper Cheese Bread, 178
Hamburger buns, 148–149
Herb Bread, 144–145
Herb rolls, 164–165
Herbs, 92
High-altitude bread baking, 119–120
High-fiber breads, 101–102
Hitachi
    HB-B101, 10
    HB-B201, 5, 11
    HB-B301, 12
Holey-textured bread, preventing, 129
Home milling, 117–118

Honey, 75–76
Hot dog buns, 148–149

I

Ingredients, 49–94
    bread machine guidelines for, 43
    dough enhancers, 81–83
    essential, 40
    fats, 72–73, 91, 97–98
    gluten, 40, 79–81
    gluten-free flours and grains, 56–57
    liquids, 40, 69–72
    measuring, 44
    miscellaneous, 87–90
    non-wheat flours, 54–55
    salt, 40, 66–67, 73, 92–93, 100–101
    sources for, 189–191
    sourdough, 84–86
    substitutions, 90–94
    sweeteners, 73–79, 93–94, 99–100
    wheat flours, 49–53
    whole grains, 58–65
    yeast, 5–6, 40, 65–69, 94, 188
Instant flour, 51
Instant yeast, 67
Internet, 113

J

"Jack-in-the-Box Syndrome, The," 45
Jaffe Bros., 190
Jalapeño Cheese Bread, 151
Jam, 4–5
Jana's Seed and Nut Bread, 154–155
J.B. Dough & Company, 191
Jessica's Biscuit, 192
Jim's Cinnamon Rolls, 146–147
Jim's Maple Walnut Bread, 152
Judging the dough, 44–46
Juice, 88

K

Kamut and kamut flour, 53, 65
Kasha, 63–64

King Arthur Flour, 190
Kneading/mixing dough, 40
Knives, 135

L

Laurel's Kitchen Bread Book, The, 82
Lecithin, 82
Legume flours, 57
Lelani bread, 150
Lemon bread, 153
Lewis, Diana, 97
Lillian Vernon, 192
Linda's Lemon Bread, 153
Liquid fruit concentrates, 78, 99
Liquids, 40, 69–72
    buttermilk, 71
    milk, 70
    miscellaneous, 71–72
    water, 69–70
Loaf shape, 2–3
Loaf size, 2
Lois's Country Crunch Bread, 162–163

M

Magic Baking Sheet, 135
Magic Mill, 191
Mail order, purchasing a machine by, 2
Malted barley flour, 81–82, 100, 103
Manual (dough) cycle, 3, 111
Maple sugar, 75
Maple syrup, 77
Maple walnut bread, 152
Margarine, 72, 91, 97–98
Maxim Accu Bakery BB-1, 17
Measurements/conversions, 47–48
Measuring ingredients, 44
Melody's Brown and White Bread
    (gluten-free), 108
Methylcellulose, 104
Miles Kimball, 192
Milk, 70
    breads without, 102–103
    substitutions for, 92, 102–103
    See also Dairy products
Milk bread, 170

Millet and millet flour, 55, 64
Milling grains, 50, 117–118
Misshapen loaves, preventing, 130–131
Mixes, bread machine, 89
Mixing/kneading dough, 40
    problems, 127
MK Seiko
    Mr. Loaf HB-12W, 13
    Mr. Loaf HB-211, 14
    Mr. Loaf HB-210, 15
    Mr. Loaf/Chefmate HB-215, 16
Molasses, 77
Multigrain breads, 160, 177
Mushroom tops, preventing, 125–126

N

Nonfat dry milk, 70
Non-wheat flours, 54–55
    amaranth, 55, 64
    barley, 55, 63
    buckwheat, 55
    millet, 55, 64
    oat, 54, 61–63
    rye, 54, 61
    storage of, 55
    teff, 55
Nut and seed bread, 154–155
Nutritional benefits of homemade bread,
    95–97
Nuts, 89

O

Oatmeal apple bread with raisins,
    143
Oatmeal Bread, 176
Oats, 61–63
    bran, 62–63
    flour, 54
    groats, 62
Oil, 72, 91
    cholesterol and saturated fat of, 98–99
    ways to reduce or eliminate, 97–98
Onion, 92
Orange whole wheat bread, 141
Oven, baking breads in, 3, 111

Oven spring, 42, 46
Overflow, preventing, 125–126

P

Packaged bread machine mixes, 89
Pale loaves, 128
Panasonic/National bread machines, 140
  SD-BT10P, 18
  SD-BT55P, 19
  SD-BT65P, 20
  yeast dispenser in, 6
Pans for baking
  baking sheets, 135–136
  nonstick, 110
  types of, 42–43
Pastry brush, 136
Pastry flour, 51
Pizza, equipment for, 137
Pizza crust, whole wheat, 174–175
Pizza dough, flattening, 41
Potassium bromate, 51, 83
Potato flours, 56
Potatoes, 89–90
Power saver, 6
Preheat cycle, 3
Problem solving, 113, 120–131
Pumpernickel rye flour, 54

Q

Quaker Multigrain Bread, 160
Quick Bake, 3
Quick breads, 4–5
Quick-Rise yeast, 67
Quinoa and quinoa flour, 57, 64–65

R

Raisin/nut cycle, 4, 112
Raisins, 90
Rapid bake cycle, 3
Rapid-Rise yeast, 67
Raw doughy spots, preventing, 127
Recipes
  adapting for bread machine, 114–115

creating your own, 116–117
Linda and Lois', 106–108, 139–185
  Anne and Bill's Apple Oatmeal Bread
    with Raisins, 143
  Ann's Bierocks, 172–173
  Applesauce Rye Bread, 171
  Bob's Cheddar Cheese Bread
    (gluten-free), 107
  Buttermilk Honey Bran Bread, 154
  Chicken Broccoli Pockets, 166–167
  Christy's Christmas Trees, 182–184
  Country Rye Bread Sticks, 180–181
  Dawn's Vanilla Raisin Bread,
    168–169
  Dede's Buttermilk Bread, 142
  Dennis's Multigrain Bread, 177
  French Bread Extraordinaire!,
    158–159
  Gene's Basic Rice Bread (gluten-free),
    106
  Ham and Pepper Cheese Bread, 178
  Herb Bread, 144–145
  Jalapeño Cheese Bread, 151
  Jana's Seed and Nut Bread, 154–155
  Jim's Cinnamon Rolls, 146–147
  Jim's Maple Walnut Bread, 152
  Linda's Lemon Bread, 153
  Lois's Country Crunch Bread,
    162–163
  Melody's Brown and White Bread
    (gluten-free), 108
  Oatmeal Bread, 176
  Quaker Multigrain Bread, 160
  San Diego Sunshine, 141
  Shareen's Whole Wheat Pizza Crust,
    174–175
  Shayna's Vegan Burgers, 156–158
  Sweet Lelani Bread, 150
  Sweet Milk Bread, 170
  Whole Wheat Hamburger and Hot
    Dog Buns, 148–149
  Whole Wheat Cinnamon Raisin
    Bread, 161
Red Star yeast, 66, 69
Refrigerating dough, 131
Regal bread machines
  K6774, 21
  Kitchen Pro K6773, 22
  K6775, 23

Resources, 192–193
Rice bread (gluten-free), 106
Rice cooking, 4–5
Rice flours, 56
Rising of dough, 40–42
  problems with, 120–124
Rolled oats, 61–62
Rye berries, 61
Rye breads
  applesauce, 171
  sour, 185
  sticks, 180–181
Rye flour, 54
Rye flakes, 61

S

Saco Buttermilk Powder, 191
Salt, 40, 66–67, 72
  cutting in half, 100–101
  substitutions for, 92–93, 101
San Diego Sunshine, 141
Sandwich breads, 186
Sanyo
  Bread Factory SBM-11, 24
  Bread Factory Plus SBM-12, 25
Seed and nut bread, 154–155
Seeds, 90
Self-rising flour, 51
Semolina flour, 53
Service, importance of, 2
Shareen's Whole Wheat Pizza Crust,
    174–175
Shayna's Vegan Burgers, 156–158
Shortening, 72, 91
Slicing bread, 112–113, 135
Small loaves, causes and solutions,
    120–124
Snacking breads, 186
Snackmaker, electric, 136
Sodium. See Salt
Soft crusts, preventing, 128
Sorghum, 65, 77
Sour cream, substitutions for, 93, 97–98
Sour rye bread, 185
Sources
  equipment and accessories, 191–192
  ingredients, 189–191

Sourdough, 84–86
  substitutions for, 93
Soy flour, 56–57
Soy milk, use of, 102–103
Spelt flour, 53
Spring wheat flour, 49
Sprouting whole grains, 58–59
Steel-cut oats, 62
Stone-ground flour, 50
Storing ingredients, 109–110
  bread, 133
  dough, 131–132
  flour, 50, 55, 57
  sweeteners, 78
  yeast, 69
Stuffing, breads for, 188
Substitutions, 90–94
Sucanat, 75
Sugar, 73–75
  brown, 74
  date, 75
  fructose, 75, 99
  maple, 75
  reducing or eliminating, 99–100
  substitutions, 93–94
  sucanat, 75
  turbinado, 75
  white, 74
  See also Sweeteners
Sunken loaves, 125
Sweet bread cycle, 4
Sweeteners, 73–78
  barley malt syrup, 78, 99,
      103
  brown rice syrup, 78, 99
  corn syrup, 77
  fructose, 75, 99
  honey, 75–76
  liquid fruit, 78, 99
  maple syrup, 77
  molasses, 77
  reducing or eliminating, 99–100
  sorghum, 77
  storage, 78
  substitutions, 93–94
  sugar, 74–75
Sweet Lelani Bread, 150
Sweet Milk Bread, 170
Sweet rice flour, 56

T

Tad Enterprises, 190
Tapioca flour, 57
Teff flour, 55
Toast, breads for, 186
Toasting whole grains, 59
Toastmaster
    Bread Box 1150, 26
    Bread Box 1151, 27
Tools
    extras, 134–138
    sources for, 191–192
Tough crust, 128
Trillium Breadman TR-500, 28
Triticale and triticale flour, 53, 64
Troubleshooting, 113, 120–131
    air bubbles, 128
    blisters, 129
    burnt crusts, 128
    coarse breads, 129
    coarse, crumbly texture, 130
    collapsed sides, 129
    cracks, 127
    crisp crusts, 129
    dry bread, 129–130
    misshapen loaves, 130–131
    mixing, 127
    overflow or mushroom tops, 125–126
    pale loaves, 128
    raw doughy spots, 127
    small loaves, 120–124
    soft crusts, 128
    sunken loaves, 125
    tough crust, 128
    yeasty flavor, 129
Turbinado sugar, 75
Turbo cycle, 3

U

Unbleached flour, 51
Universal Foods Corporation, 189

V

Vanilla raisin bread, 168–169
Vegan burgers, 156–158

Vegetable broth, 71–72
Vegetables and fruits, 72, 91
Vegetarians, breads for, 102–103
Viewing window, 5
Vital wheat gluten and vital wheat gluten
    flour, 79–80
Von Snadaker's "Magic Baking Sheet,"
    135

W

Walnut Acres, 191
Water, 69–70
Weather, breads and, 46, 118–119
Weight loss, bread and, 96
Welbilt bread machines
    ABM 100, 29
    ABM 150R Multilogic, 30
    ABM 300/350, 31
    ABM 500/550, 32
    ABM 600, 33
    ABM 800, 34
West Bend Bread and Dough Maker
    #41030, 35
    #41040, 36
Wheat bran, 59
Wheat berries, 49, 59
Wheat flakes, 60
Wheat flours, 49–53
    all-purpose, 50
    bread, 49, 51
    cake/pastry, 51
    durum, 53
    graham, 53
    instant, 51
    kamut, 53, 65
    self-rising, 51
    semolina, 53
    spelt, 53
    triticale, 53, 64
    unbleached, 51
    whole wheat, 50–52
Wheat-free breads, 104–108
    recipes, 106–108
Wheat germ, 60
White flour, 50
White whole wheat flour, 52
Whole grains, 58–65

amaranth, 64
barley, 63
bulgur, 59
cornmeal, 63
cracked rye, 61
cracked wheat, 59
kamut, 65
kasha, 63–64
millet, 64
oat bran, 62–63
oat groats, 62
quinoa, 64–65
rolled oats, 61–62
rye berries, 61
rye flakes, 61
sorghum, 65
steel-cut oats, 62
triticale, 64
wheat berries, 59
wheat bran, 59
wheat flakes, 60
wheat germ, 59
Whole wheat berries, 49, 59
Whole Wheat Cinnamon Raisin Bread,
    161
Whole wheat cycle, 4
Whole wheat flakes, 60
Whole wheat flours, 50–52, 52
  substitutions for, 94
Whole Wheat Hamburger and Hot Dog
    Buns, 148–149
Whole wheat orange bread, 141

Whole wheat pizza crust, 174–175
Wholesale-by-Mail Catalogue, The, 2
Winter wheat flour, 49
Wonderslim, 97
Wooden Spoon, The, 192

X

Xanthan gum, 104

Y

Yeast, 40, 65–69
  active dry, 67
  activity of, 68
  compressed (fresh), 68
  fast-acting, 67–68
  fermentation process and, 66–67
  storage of, 69
  substitutions, 94
Yeast dispenser, 6
Yeasty flavor, preventing, 129

Z

Zest, 88–89, 135–136
Zojirushi Home Bakery
  BBCC-N15, 37
  BBCC-S15, 38

You can obtain additional copies of this book, or the authors' best-selling cookbook *Bread Machine Magic*, at your local bookseller, or by using the coupon below.

ORDER FORM
Please send me the following books:

——— copies of *The Bread Machine Magic Book of Helpful Hints*
(ISBN 0-312-09759-X $10.95)
——— copies of *Bread Machine Magic*
(ISBN 0-312-06914-6 $10.95)

Enclosed is a check or money order, payable to Publishers Book & Audio, in the amount of $——— (please include shipping and handling charges of $3.00 for the first book, and $1.00 for each additional book).

Send books to: Name _____

Address _____

_____

_____

Send this coupon and your payment to: Publishers Book & Audio, P.O. Box 070059, Staten Island, New York 10307. Please allow four to six weeks for delivery.

For bulk orders (10 or more copies), contact St. Martin's Press, Special Markets Division, 175 Fifth Avenue, New York, NY 10010. Or call, toll free, 1–800–221–7945, extension #645.